Far in
Far out

A collection of essays on Inner Work

The Research Society for
Process Oriented Psychology U.K.

Impressum

The Research Society for Process Oriented Psychology U.K.
(RSPOPUK)
213 Haverstock Hill
London
NW3 4NG

e-mail contact@rspopuk.com
www.rspopuk.com

First Published 2006
ISBN 978-1-84728-671-0

*Book Publication Team: Gina Clayton, Anup Karia, Stanya
Studentova, Louise Warner, Kirsten Wassermann*

Cover image & design by Helen Wells
Book design & layout by Kirsten Wassermann

Printed by www.lulu.com

Pour notre cher ami, Jean-Claude, avec amour.
Nous remercions l'esprit qui nous a réunis.

For our dear friend, Jean-Claude Audergon with love.
We thank the spirit that brought us together.

Contents

Preface

We dedicate this book to Jean-Claude Audergon with deepest gratitude and love for his impeccable teaching and continual eldership. No gift can truly express our gratitude for his tireless fostering of awareness in us and in the world.

Jean-Claude is a co-developer of Process Work (with Arnold Mindell and colleagues) and also a co-founder of the Process Work schools in Zurich, Portland and the UK. He is a teacher, supervisor and a mentor for students in the UK and internationally, an organisational consultant and international conflict facilitator. He also works with individual clients and with artists.

The idea for this book was conceived in a loud London pub where some of us, students of Process Work, had gathered on a cold spring evening; we were excited in our ponderings of how to celebrate Jean-Claude's 60th birthday later in the year. Many suggestions came and went and then we thought about a book where all of us could contribute. …This felt the right thing to do as it would challenge us way beyond our normal identities as most of us don't identify as writers! One of Jean-Claude's favourite sayings came to mind: 'The edge is a far out place, it is a place of growing'. We immediately thought of a title: 'Far in, Far out', as it represents the journey inside, as well as staying deeply connected out in the world.

The topic of Inner Work emerged from what we felt was Jean-Claude's biggest teaching and modelling to us:

opening ourselves to what is happening in every moment. According to Arnold Mindell the inner self, relationships and the world are all aspects of the same collective process. In this sense Inner Work means working on the inner or outer situation as reflections in one's inner life and is the central awareness method in Process Work. The pages that follow will demonstrate to you examples of Inner Work and its use in different contexts including with self, in relationships, within organisations and in the wider world. There are also personal tributes to Jean Claude-Audergon. For the most part, Process Work terms are explained. For any further clarification the reader is referred to the glossary at www.maxfacilitation.net.

The experience of bringing this book to birth has been an exciting and challenging one. Individual contributors have worked deeply on themselves right the way through the process. Some thirty people have written, composed, painted or photographed to make a contribution to the book.

All of us have been working with the paradox of the creative process: our passionate energy and the constraints of timescales and publishing. For the book production team this was exemplified in the question of how to order the pieces in the book. The team did a piece of collective Inner Work, in a pub car park in Norwich, to help us resolve the question. There we were, five of us, walking dreamily around with our eyes closed and following ourselves. What emerged was a remarkable unanimity of lightness and naturalness. We abandoned our previous ideas, and a sense emerged that the pieces would go in an order which their individual qualities suggested. The qualities of each would show which piece would be a natural companion, follower or a contrast. May this book be an inspiration for you, the reader, as the production was an invitation to a creative journey for us.

Acknowledgements

Thank you Arnold & Amy Mindell and colleagues for continually discovering and developing the whole field of Process Work. This book rests on all of your shoulders.

We thank Arlene Audergon for her dream about the creation of RSPOPUK community. From the bottom of our hearts we also thank all those who continually help the dream to manifest.

Deep appreciation to all the contributors who are drawn from the diverse UK and international Process Work communities for sharing of themselves in this way and for devoting time in their busy schedules at such short notice. Gratitude also to all the unnamed people who were supporting the contributors through encouragement, feedback and giving their resources towards the production of the book.

We want to acknowledge and thank the Editorial Committee of the RSPOPUK for their support, and particularly Edna Holt, Mark O'Connell, Sally Olsberg, Helen Wells and Evelyn Figueroa for their loving and detailed reading and feedback on all the contributions.

The publication team has had an exciting time as the five of us stepped into these roles not knowing what this would entail. We have been learning on the hoof about many aspects of producing an edited collection for publiccation. It has been an immense privilege for us. Thanks to everyone for their confidence in us and support.

So, Jean-Claude, while this book began as a gift to you, in the end once more you gave a gift to all of us: the gift of creating, struggling and learning together from the heart. This has fostered a sense of community for all of us.
- Far out! -

Gina Clayton, Anup Karia, Stanya Studentova, Louise Warner and Kirsten Wassermann
Book Publication Team
July 2006

Foreword

The Facilitator's Inner Work in the Outer World

It makes us happy to celebrate Jean-Claude Audergon's sixtieth birthday by honoring his greatest gift: studying himself, tracking his own inner experiences while helping to facilitate real world issues in individual therapy and in the midst of social issues in large groups.

He models the Process Work paradigm in his own individual manner, realizing the nonlocality, that is, the power of the human field to penetrate and touch everything and everyone in it. Because of this magnetic human field, facilitators are moved about in themselves relative to their own inner parts and to the parts of their organisations. While the more conventional facilitator tries to manage situations, sorting out real issues and helping people in everyday reality to meet according to the game plans of various communication methods, Process Work, while affirming these methods goes a step further. A Process Worker knows that the world of social reality, the business and organisational community world is at the same time both a very real world of facts and figures, and a world of deep feelings and dreams, experiences no one dares to truly know or explore.

While most of us hesitate at the brink of everyday life's outer drama, Jean-Claude models (as do some other process people), just how to go deeper below the surface. He models how to work on himself personally and publicly to elucidate not only personal experience but also the general processes touching everyone and everything in the field at that moment.

This Process Work attitude, this 'inner awareness work for outer consciousness' is similar to that of the shaman who goes into altered states of consciousness for the benefit of her community. She divines its dreams, its visions, its problems and eventually, its solutions.

So we are so thankful to Jean-Claude and to those who contributed to this book, for their various insights and stories about how to understand the inner nature of the facilitator who works to make outer life better for all.

May this book help and inspire anyone needing motivation and wanting to know how and what to do with inner life in the outer world.

Amy and Arny Mindell, Ph.D.'s
Portland Oregon, USA
June 2006

Becoming Zorro

By Charleen Agostini

I recall a time not so long ago when I was longing for something but didn't know what I was longing for. I decided to do some Inner Work. Inner Work involves focussing on a chosen issue or disturbance and tracking how it manifests and unfolds in both inner and outer experiences.

As I walked around my house with the intent of addressing my longing, my attention was caught by a crumpled piece of paper on the floor. It was a screwed-up a piece of paper thrown away that had missed the bin. This screwed-up paper was 'flirting' with me which means something about it was asking for my notice and attention. I dropped my ordinary way of looking at it and allowed it to speak to me as though it were significant. The more I looked at it the more I could understand how that piece of paper felt. I then remembered a dream of the night before where I was a refugee.

Yes – I knew that feeling in myself where I feel excluded, discarded, unloved. No place for me! But who was doing the excluding and what exactly was being excluded? As that piece of paper it felt that it was the world and most everyone I knew. Calling on the part of me that is open to my wholeness I decided to become the crumpled piece of paper on the floor to find out more about its nature from its point of view.

Dry – brittle, sharp at the edges! I certainly did not identify with being like that. This felt like a threat to my way of being with people in the world and the need I have to be the warm woman I am, and to love and be loved by others. Could it really be true that I have a part of me that is dry and sharp, and because of that I have tried to bin it? Yes. My every-day self felt it would be very difficult to keep the love-thing going in my relationships with such a dry and sharp way of being. But doing this means having to live an apartheid in myself. Yes! I have to maintain a totalitarian regime in myself. This is the only way to keep the status quo.

In the meantime I suffer, through my longing and a body full of physical aches and pains. I am caught in this and do not know the way out. I am the refugee *and* the country that makes people flee.

Noticing that I also long for a world where these painful polarities do not dominate in this way, I call upon those parts of me that are able to stand outside polarities wherever I might find them – inside or outside me, and decide to delve a bit deeper into the nature of the dry sharp way of being. At this point I am both outside my process as an Elder, the one who cares for the whole, and experiencing the parts of my nature that seem foreign.

As I identify as a person who is dry and sharp I begin to feel like someone who is more able to say things and not be concerned with what others think or feel. Someone who comes out with things and is not concerned if it disturbs. I become more interested in noticing how things are than noticing the effect the noticing has on others. I am more unrelated and detached. My attention goes on saying what is happening rather than on being careful about how I say what I say. It is both scary and a great relief.

As I identify with this more and more I get very excited because I begin to discover a part of me that is a detached thinker rather than a feeler! - So foreign! - A shock! - Exciting! I feel a sense of freedom and euphoria. Freedom of thought! Not bound by protocol or ideas of right or wrong. A freedom to think the unthinkable and feel the unfeelable. I feel a little bit crazy as I am momentarily freed from needing to fit in to everyday reality. The 'refugee' feels free to be herself in her new country.

Not for long though as my everyday self reacts against my recently discovered freedom to behave without so much sensitivity to those around me. Now a big work starts on how to welcome and envision these parts living together in the same neighbourhood with different cultural beliefs and views on life. My inner world reflects the problems of the outer world.

As I go deeper into the nature of the sharp, detached, dry part of myself I reconnect to a recurring childhood dream where I am being chased by a man in a cloak with a bullwhip. I recognise this process having worked on this night-time dream many times before and realise that the discarded, crumpled piece of paper that first flirted with me this day is part of my life myth, appearing in a different form, indicating my need to again address this process in myself. I can immediately reconnect to this process – I call it 'Becoming Zorro' – the being who is so skilled at using a bull-whip that he can remove the shirt on someone without his whip touching the skin. For me he embodies both the sensitive loving part and the accurate, detached, sharp way of being. I am thankful for having Zorro as a meaningful embodiment and dream of where I am heading, as this will be an ongoing life work for me.

When I was asked to write something for Jean-Claude to be put into a book I immediately hit a feeling and belief in myself that said: 'That is impossible in the time with all the other pressures.' *'impossible'* – hey - that sounds fitting for Jean-Claude. Yes, it is something about the impossible made possible that happens with you Jean-Claude.

Time and time again – over the years – millenniums possibly – we meet across the phone lines mainly, where you Jean-Claude teach me how to facilitate myself here in the day-to-day Tonal[1] life, sourced in the Nagual[2]. Your heart and humanness coupled with detachment and ruthlessness helps me walk this path.

I reach out with love and gratefulness to you as my Teacher, Shaman, Mentor, Friend, Colleague. I thank you with all my heart and soul for being who you are for sharing your life and wisdom.

Charleen Agostini
is a certified Process Worker, Mother and Grandmother. She lives and works in Bristol. She has recently been focussing on working with a small team on setting up Open Forums to address Diversity Issues.

[1] Tonal refers to our ordinary everyday state of consciousness and reality.

[2] Nagual means the living unconscious, the unknown, non-consensus reality, and altered states of reality.

Mixing it up
Process Work Applied in Music Production

By Gareth Williams

A dream from several years ago:

I'm sitting in a small church where one of my favourite guitarists is giving a concert. After playing his electric guitar for a short while, he puts it down and begins to make music with the sound effects unit that the signal from his instrument is being processed by. His fingers press the buttons and move the dials with the same speed and dexterity he plays the guitar. Amazing sounds, rich in texture and tone emerge. Surrounded by these sounds I find myself going deeper and deeper into a very altered state of consciousness. No longer seated in the small church, I am I know not where. It's a mixture of scary, exciting and blissful.

I began experimenting with music technology in my early 20s with a very basic computer and sampler (digital recorder capable of manipulating audio material) with a memory holding about half a minute of sounds (the sampler, not me!). My current studio set up still remains very modest (by industry standards) but now, due to developments in technology and personal income, I have enough memory for about half a week! I sold my first studio after a couple of years to pursue community work and studies of shamanism. Since taking on a youth work job 5 years ago, I have once again been involved with recording and production. I have probably made in excess of 200 recordings over this time with a diversity of young people, both those who would and would not identify them-selves as musicians. It has been a lot of fun and proven to be a most effective bridge for making contact and exploring a wide range of experiences and issues.

One of my current interests is in finding ways to weave together my love of music production with my love of Process Work. The compact disc included with this book is the first public presentation of my personal exploration into the meeting point of these two disciplines. It is my hope that the listener will at least find it interesting and at best be transported into another world as I was in the dream recounted above.

What characterises a Process-Oriented approach to music production? Welcoming the unintended and a willingness to venture into the unknown; awareness of edges[1] and supporting people around them; taking guidance from environmental and internal feedback; ability to work in a variety of channels[2], not just in the auditory; openness to the essential dimension of experience; and facilitating interaction between all members of a project or all parts of a person. Add to this the qualities of playfulness, patience, trust and not forcing things to turn out a parti-cular way, and we're on our way to an image of a Process Work producer, as well as a long list! Different skills and attitudes will be called forth at different times, with each practitioner undertaking a recording session based on their personal uniqueness and the uniqueness of the particular situation. It is likely that many music producers work in ways that could be described as Process-Oriented without naming it as such, using some of the aforementioned skills and meta-skills[3]. Perhaps what would set a Process Worker apart would be awareness of what he or she is doing and a certain language and framework in which to operate.

It is generally recognised in the music industry that some producers rely upon a studio engineer to operate the equipment. This being the case, it means any Process Worker with the interest, motivation and opportunity could take on the role of producer.

The piece on the accompanying disc began on a Saturday in May 2006 during a supervision group facilitated by Sally Olsberg. My fellow supervisees and supervisor were very generous in their willingness to travel to my studio and I'd like to thank them for their interest, energy and support. After welcoming everyone to my studio space, I quickly introduced the recording equipment and outlined some of my ideas. I made it clear that I was very open to whatever would emerge and encouraged people to feel very free to experiment with whatever sounds interested them.

We recorded 3 tracks: (1) a synthesiser sound emulating the sound of tinnitus (a symptom experienced by several members of the group); (2) a 15 minute recording of the whole group improvising together with voice and percussion instruments; and (3) a review of our recording session. Tracks 1 and 2 were recorded simultaneously. Track 3 was recorded immediately upon completion of 1 and 2.

Following this, over the following weeks, I listened through the recordings and allowed myself to follow ideas and sounds that flirted[4] with me. Some (maybe all) of these sounds/passages were, in effect, dream doors[5] and opened up avenues of exploration and development. Other sounds I used in a more planned way for added effect and to enhance the listening experience. Which part of me is producing? The shaman? The one seeking praise and recognition? The perfectionist? The musician with an agreed code of tempo and tuning? Who else is in me controlling the faders and editing the tracks? Reflecting upon these questions as I worked, I found all of these aspects of myself guiding the production process. In the spirit of deep democracy, I allowed each aspect to arise, take the controls, make their contribution and then move aside to make room for the next contributor. In one moment I am Experimenter with Fate and Chance, randomly importing guitar tracks into the mix, in the next, I am Perfectionist-Producer, trying to fine-tune the tone and then get the length of the piece just right. Increased awareness of the complexity and diversity of who I am as a producer allowed me to more fully express all the different parts of myself in the creative process.

The high-pitched sound in the background throughout the piece is my attempt to create the hissing-ringing that has been accompanying me through a large portion of my waking experience during the past few years. It is not entirely accurate but a very close emulation.

One of my ideas for a few future project is a 'Symptom Symphony' or 'Symptony', where auditory symptoms and-or sonic amplifications of symptoms in other channels can be blended together to create a piece of sound art. For now, however, I am happy to say how much I enjoyed exploring music production in a process-oriented style and I look forward to discovering more sounds that emerge from my own and other people's experiences. So forget the sound of one hand clapping and listen to the sound of your exper-ience rapping!

Copies of **the Far Out music** piece, '**Never Stop**', are available

either in MP3 format at http://www.myspace.com/faroutproject or direct from Gareth on CD for a small charge. by email at peacemanproject@hotmail.co.uk.

Currently a Process Work student, **Gareth Williams** has an undergraduate degree in Psychology, a masters degree in Music and a diploma in Person-Centred Counselling. He works for a charity supporting and promoting the well-being of young people through counselling and music. Gareth has a lifelong passion for making music, playing guitar, bass, percussion and, more recently, using his voice. His postgraduate studies focused upon shamanism.

[1]   Edges can be thought of as the perceived limits of our identity, intentionality and awareness. Beyond the edge lies experience and parts of ourselves that we don't recognise as being the 'typical me' or 'what I do'.

[2]   Process Work differentiates a number of channels in which information-experience can flow and unfold: visual, auditory, proprioceptive (felt sensations), kinaesthetic (movement), relationship and world.

[3]   Metaskills are conscious attitudes that inform how we do what we do. For example, guitar playing techniques (such as chords, scales and strumming styles) are skills. The way I utilise the skills (adventurously, sensitively, or with detachment) are the metaskills.

[4]   Something flirts with a person when it catches his or her interest/attention.

[5]   Dream doors are experiences that, if given time and attention, can be a springboard into altered states of consciousness and meaningful learning.

I have had Tinnitus...

By Emily Hodgkinson

I have had tinnitus for many years now and through Process Work I have been lucky to move beyond the experience of being only a victim of tinnitus, towards feeling privileged to have constant contact with this incredible vibration. At times I do feel like a victim.....when I'm standing on a hilltop and I cannot hear the silence...when I'm out in the fields and my friend can hear birdsong that I cannot.....when lying in bed at night unable to listen to the sound of rain on the window panes. But the non-consensual reality of my tinnitus is also an amazing and beautiful sound. Over the years I have worked with this sound and discovered more about my own qualities of continuity and determination and the never-ending flow of life and energy within me that has taken me on journeys I once thought impossible, and will take me as far as I can dream. My constant tinnitus reminds me of my own inability to give up on my dreams, on myself, on my relationships and my hopes for the world. It is also a constant reminder of my ability to be in touch with the dreaming world, to hear messages from spirits and gods.

One of the harder aspects of living within a non-consensual auditory reality is the isolation, the fact of not being able to share my experience with others, or to fully share in their soundscapes. The most surprising, healing aspect of this tinnitus project was, for me, that for the brief time it took for us to make and record these sounds, I did not 'have tinnitus' – my hearing experience was the same reality as those around me. I did not 'have a hearing problem'. My inner auditory world was made real.

Emily Hodgkinson
Participant in the 'tinnitus' music project.
She is a phase 2 student of Process Work and an earth scientist. She is currently researching behaviour around environmental issues from a process-oriented perspective.

Light and Dark, Kirsten Wassermann

In the Margins

By Pat Black

Introduction

As I sit down to write an article about Inner Work as a contribution to a book being compiled to celebrate one of my great teachers, Jean-Claude Audergon, I am struggling to work out what to write. My learning from Jean-Claude has been about many things. At the moment I am concentrating on the discipline of applying Inner Work to everything, in fact even writing 'applying' seems to diminish the depth of my learning about its importance. In Process Work, Inner Work is at the heart of all of the work and the patient, generous and loving teaching of that by example, demonstration, challenge and a painstaking attention to theory and practice has been a part of the gift I have received from Jean Claude during my supervision sessions with him and in seminars.

One of the difficulties I have had in describing Inner Work is a belief system that assumes because the practice of Inner Work is internal to oneself and, by its nature, very personal, it is somehow self indulgent or individualist in its intent and not therefore directly useful to any of the people with whom I am working. Part of my learning has been understanding that not only is it a necessary and invaluable practice for me as an individual but it has made my teaching and facilitation of individual and group work more useful to the participants. Because you are able to go deeply inside yourself in the moment you can become more available to others and more effective in your work, whatever it is.

So, as I write, this is also the challenge of the learning to do Inner Work right now and make that useful in my writing; I notice that I want to be distracted, watch birds, do the garden anything but write and so I decide to go into that feeling and be really distracted. I stand up from the chair and move to the window to really look out and in doing that and staying with the looking and then imagining more deeply into that figure (the one who is looking out) and what is at the essence of it[1] it is as if I step into the figure of a large and compassionate god who has her arms folded and looks at me working and says "really look at what you are doing" and "write the story that wants to be told". And now I know what to write.

I am going to write about my work with one man and tell a little of his story and where my Inner Work was useful to him. The Inner Work and other work I did with him and the organisation supporting him was supervised and supported by Jean- Claude.

The story

This is the story of a man I will call Malcolm; it is a hard story to tell because although he is in his 40s he has not had the same life opportunities as most other men of his age, and has had few positive experiences to look back on as well as little to look forward to. He was 42 when I met him eighteen months ago (in 2005) and he was living in a group home with 5 other men. He was described as violent to himself and others and has a label of a learning disability[2] and Downs Syndrome. Malcolm does not speak. The environment in which he was living was shocking. He had lived there with the same people for over 14 years. Malcolm had lived with his parents and brothers until he was 15 then his father died and his mother felt unable to cope, his brothers had left home by that time and although in touch did not live nearby.

He was placed in a large hospital for people with learning disabilities; his Mum stayed in close contact but died a few years later. It is unlikely that he was told that his Mum had died, so from his perspective she may just have stopped visiting. He stayed in that hospital for 13 years until it was closed. When various organisations selected people to move on he was never chosen, he had a reputation for challenging behaviour and was not wanted by any group. So, when the hospital closed he, and the other half dozen or so people who were not wanted, were put together and supported by hospital employees in a house on the outskirts of a very small, very expensive village, where they were not wanted by the village.

It was cold and bare, the internal doors to most rooms were locked and all 6 of the men spent most of their time in the narrow hallway walking up and down or waiting to get into the locked kitchen for a cup of tea. The staff members were mainly in the office or the kitchen and there was little interaction between them and the men except at mealtimes or when an outing was being organised. Malcolm rarely went out, usually he was not allowed to go because his behaviour earlier in the day would have been 'bad' and he would be being punished by not being allowed out. He spent most of the time in the hallway sitting on the floor shivering and cold, he would often have taken off most of the clothes he had been wearing, sometimes he would scream or lie on the floor and hit himself.

We know from the many stories of people surviving long stay hospitals that abuse and neglect are common place and it is likely that Malcolm was abused. At the very least he moved from a warm and loving family to an institution and lost all outside contacts over the first few years. We also know that people who do not use words are very likely to experience sexual abuse[3] and because they are unable to tell anyone exactly what is happening it is rarely prevented or people prosecuted. Most people in this situation have to use their behaviour to demonstrate their unhappyness and as they are rarely taken seriously in large scale institutions many people will self harm or become violent towards others. Often people are treated for their behaviour without the cause of their unhappiness being considered.

The house where he lived was to be closed because it did not meet any of the required standards and my colleague and partner, Andy Smith, and I were engaged to work out what sorts of supported living arrangements would work for each of the individual men. We worked this out one person at a time and in collaboration with families or others who knew and loved or cared about them. Malcolm had no one to ask, no one liked him and no one appeared to know anything personal about him even though some staff had been around him for over 20 years.

Alongside the more usual process of person centred planning[4] we used our knowledge of Process Work and particularly Inner Work to work with Malcolm. Because this is a complex piece of work operating on many levels over a period of time I am only going to describe three examples that I hope will illustrate how useful Inner Work is in this sort of setting.

Example 1

Firstly, we were very distressed at the environment and the way in which people were being treated and we used our external supervision sessions to explore some of these feelings. I noticed that I kept feeling that I should give the staff the benefit of the doubt and that I should not say to them my real feelings about what was happening around Malcolm. In my supervision session I explained the set up and commented on how physically cold I was feeling. Jean-Claude encouraged me to feel the cold even more and become it, at the essence of the cold was a detached figure that could be direct and could also bring in feelings, especially feelings of distress without worrying about upsetting others.

On one level, my primary identity[5] was to be useful, to do a good job and to be polite and not upset anyone. When I explored some of what was more secondary[6] to me, I realised that it was to be coldly detached and I had an edge[7] to being direct with staff and bringing in my own distress. Becoming aware of this edge in myself helped us then to understand that one of the many edges in the system was to allow feelings, particularly of distress, to be openly expressed and explored, the distress of the people supported and the distress of some of the staff were marginalised and largely ignored.

Internally for me this edge connected to belief systems of my own about not being wanted if you show feelings, especially of distress, and this links to the system in several ways: the myth that the house and its occupants were 'not wanted'; that Malcolm (and the others) were not wanted when they showed feelings of distress, the main staff procedure when Malcolm showed distress, which was to withhold attention and say "we don't want you to come out with us if you do that". As I used Inner Work to became more aware about my own personal areas of challenge in working in this situation the information also helped me to become aware of some of the system edges and difficulties and it had a ripple effect as sharing this awareness with others in the system allowed further unfolding of the distress felt by many of the individuals (staff and service users).

This is one example of the use of Inner Work at the beginning of a piece of work, the information then needs to be made available back into the organisation in ways that can be understood and unfolded by the people involved. The first step for me was to directly bring in my feelings, particularly of distress and enable others to do the same.

Example 2

This example is of using Inner Work to guide our direct communication with Malcolm. I began by using Inner Work to attend to what I was feeling in his company and to find out what that told me about how to be with him.

When I stood beside or near to him and really felt into the experience I was nervous, in a heightened way, very sensitive, serious, attentive and very astute. Reflecting on this inner experience and believing that it is connected to Malcolm as well as being a part of me I decided to take the feelings seriously and use them to guide my interaction with Malcolm. Also connecting with the awareness above about the marginalisation of feelings Andy and I decided to be completely direct with Malcolm, we decided to do Inner Work in his presence and talk about it at the same time. We decided to use sensitivity, seriousness and attentiveness as our metaskills[8]; in practice we wanted to take ourselves, each other and Malcolm seriously and completely attend to everything that was happening and report on it to him.

Andy and I started to talk out loud to each other after each internally reflecting on what was happening. Malcolm was sitting on the floor further down the hallway. We said, "we're going to talk about being here Malcolm and what we think might be happening; you can join us at any time". We talked for a while, reporting congruently on what was happening for each of us internally, about how being sensitive in this setting is really hard, and how difficult it is to have a lot of feelings about what happens but then not to take them seriously. We then also spoke about him saying we thought that Malcolm was very sensitive and that we would like to take his feelings really seriously and that we thought he had a lot to say. We spoke slowly with lots of pauses because we were both really feeling into what we said and trying to stay with our deepest internal experience. There were at least two reasons for this, firstly we did not want to try to get Malcolm to respond or engage in any particular way, his usual experience is that people engage with him in order to get him to do something. Instead we wanted to be available for contact but make sure he was in control of that. Secondly people who do not use words are often very fast and skilled at noticing and responding to 'double signals'[9] rather than the information that we think we are giving. One way to stay more congruent and reduce double signalling is to stay very close to your own internal process. This means that the communication to Malcolm is likely to be clearer than usual if we are able to stay close to our own internal experience.

We spoke for about 10 minutes and he gradually edged down the hall to stand next to me and took my hands and placed them firmly on his shoulders. We continued to talk about what was happening and I reported on the detail e.g. the firmness of his touch and said also how I felt reassured by his closeness and then as I felt a need to move I said that and moved my hands from his shoulders. We stayed standing close together until after a minute or so he moved a few feet away. We all stood quietly together until it felt like time to move away. We said we were moving away but would be around in the building for the rest of the day and most of the next few days.

Next day he came up right away and leaned against me very firmly. I said that having thought about yesterday I wondered if I could check a few things out with him; he settled beside me both of us looking straight ahead. I gave him my leather jacket and a soft scarf and asked him if he liked the feel of them. He smiled when he touched the jacket and when I passed him the scarf I could feel his discomfort; he could barely touch it. I talked to him about the feel of fabrics and told him my hypothesis that some fabrics and types of touch were horrible to him and that we would make sure he didn't have to have them any more. This meant explaining to his key worker that some kinds of light touch and the feel of some fabrics is very unpleasant to him and letting him choose clothes that he liked the feel of rather then dressing him in things chosen for him that he immediately took off. We also suggested other ways of ensuring firm touch rather than light touch when supporting him.

This practical step was small but confirmed to Malcolm that we were taking him seriously and modelled using our experience of being with him to inform practical changes that could make his life more tolerable.

Example 3

This last example is slightly different; it is about the spontaneous use of Inner Work. I was talking to a staff member in Malcolm's presence about the importance of knowing that communication was not only about words and as I spoke I felt tearful and suddenly thought about a man I knew who told me about the horrific abuse he experienced in a learning disability hospital and how that had affected how he communicated. Taking this seriously as an indicator of some field effect around Malcolm as well as useful information for the conversation and for myself I told Malcolm and Sandra that I was feeling upset and checking internally with myself slowly said that I knew many people who had been hurt in hospitals, Malcolm stopped moving around and came over. I said I wondered if he had been hurt and he started to cry. I felt very sad and sorry and I said so and apologised for him having been hurt and we stayed close together for a few minutes, both of us crying. It was a very powerful and deep experience: I had apologised to him from myself and as a member of a society that had stood by while he was neglected and abused, I also promised him that we would make sure he was no longer forgotten.

Keeping the promise

When we had completed the planning processes for all of the men new services were negotiated for each of them with a small local provider. Malcolm now has his own warm and welcoming flat where he lives alone supported by a small staff team (4 people) providing one to one support 24 hours a day[10]. His life is changing all the time and he is learning about living in the outside world. Everything is not perfect and sometimes he gets upset and angry but this happens less and less as he and his team are getting to know each other, he has not hurt himself or anyone else since he moved. There are fantastic stories of his growth and development and of the fun he and his team are having as they all learn together. He loves his flat and is just beginning to relax and understand that it his place and he does not have to go back to any institution.

Most importantly he is no longer unwanted and forgotten; he is just starting to have a place in the world with people around who like him and care about him, he is beginning to experience the sense of belonging that we all need.

Conclusion

I have used Malcolm's story to give examples of the use of Inner Work in complex situations with a person who does not use words. These are some examples from many hours spent in his company and I hope they illustrate the usefulness of connecting our own internal worlds with the wider system and the external and internal worlds of others. There are many varied reasons for the disciplined and systematic use of Inner Work. One that I think is particularly important in the field of working with people who have been marginalised because of learning disability labels or because they do not speak is to enhance and deepen our ability to communicate congruently. I have had the great privilege of spending lots of time learning from people who skilfully convey and understand the deeper meaning of interactions without relying on words and practising Inner Work is one of the ways in which I too can get better at this.

Pat Black

is a student of Process Work and has worked for over 30 years in the field of disability, first training as an occupational therapist and then providing and managing services for people labelled as challenging. She has been engaged for the last 15 years in changing service provision in Scotland and in setting up innovative services. She is co-director of Diversity Matters which works with individuals, staff, families and organisations to promote service and cultural change.

[1] Essence or sentient level, for more detail see Diamond, J and Jones, L.S. (2004) *A Path Made by Walking* p.117 Portland, Oregon: LaoTse Press

[2] Learning disability is the term used in the UK to describe people with intellectual or developmental disabilities

[3] 'Sexual Abuse of people with developmental disabilities' by Nora J. Balderian in *Sexuality and Disability*, Publisher: Springer Netherlands, ISSN: 0146-1044 (Paper) 1573-6717 (Online) DOI: 10.1007/BF01102020, Vol. 9, n. 4, Dec. 1991, p. 323-335

[4] For more information see Jack Pearpoint at www.inclusion.com

[5] Primary: clear definitions are given on p 20 *A Path Made By Walking* see n. 1

[6] Secondary: as above, p.20

[7] Edge: as above, p.20

[8] Metaskills: see Mindell, Amy, (2003) *Metaskills: the spiritual art of therapy* Portland, Oregon: Lao Tse Press

[9] Double signals: ,Diamond and Jones 2004 Chapter 2. n 1 above

[10] Examples of this type of service are described in Fitzpatrick, J. 2006. 'Dreaming for Real: The Development of Partners for Inclusion' *Journal of Integrated Care*, 14 (1) February 2006 pp27-34

The Dance of Shiva
Two Conversations on Love and Inner Work

By Anup Karia and Stanya Studentova

It's a cloudy rainy afternoon in London and we are sitting in Stanya's front room sipping tea and contemplating what to write about. Jean Claude's spirit, his devotion to and love of people and their growth, is around and guiding us in this process. We notice how writing together in this way is a unique experience; and what sustains us is the love we have for each other in our friendship; how we support and challenge each other to get interested in our inner worlds and how they relate to the outside world we are part of[1]. This is what we want to write about. How love is a prerequisite to looking inside of oneself; love and the interest to go in[2].

The two conversations below emerged from our dialogues and Inner Work together. Many times we did not know who was who, that was part of the fun. By Inner Work we mean working on oneself alone to develop fluidity between inner and outer events and connect with one's creativity and spirituality.

Stanya: When I think about Inner Work I think of self-loving. It's an act of love to be interested in myself.

Anup: Beautiful! Including that which is disturbing or which I don't want to know; to consider that everything I notice around me or inside of me (even the unknown or hardly noticeable things) is me. The disturbance in me in this moment is the conflict between wanting to write about this and feeling private about it.

Stanya: Yeah – It feels like exposing something tender; it's a taboo to write about love publicly. I'm interested. It feels like a good moment to do Inner Work.

Anup: So I'll go more into what is disturbing; the need to be private.

Anup makes a gesture of holding a baby. He unfolds the movement further and discovers the deeper quality: the acute sensitivity. Through this Inner Work we realise we need to write with acute sensitivity.

Stanya: Talking openly about the hesitations makes me feel freer to write about love publicly. It's a private and a collective process.

First conversation:
Shiva: God of Perception

'Look, look: You Have Nothing Else To Do'[3] *J. Krishnamurti*

Anup: As we talk about going into disturbances with love, I am reminded of Shiva, the god of perception. In Hindu cosmology, Shiva is the one who sees all; not only sees all, but sees with adoration. A myth comes to mind: *Shiva as the supreme being of the universe gets restless in his abode on the mountain top. He escapes into the jungle and takes the form of a wild stag and lives amongst the other creatures. He has a wild old time! Meanwhile, the other gods and goddesses miss Shiva desperately and go to the jungle to get him back. Shiva refuses, and a mighty fight ensues. The stag is killed and Shiva returns back to his abode and reigns with the wildness of the stag! This is the horned god manifestation of Shiva.* To me, this myth describes the Inner Work journey: going into the jungle, embodying the disturbing experience, and getting to know

40

it from within. The fight is the interaction between the different parts and how to live the energy of the disturbance in everyday life.

Stanya: The idea of embracing and living the energy or the essence of all, even disturbing, experiences is great and speaks to my heart. The challenge comes to really live it. My teenage resistance is the disturbing aspect.

Anup: I love the teenager in you, and you are also a pain in the butt when you are challenging.

Stanya: That touches me what you say; I feel loved in my wholeness. You are Shiva in this moment. Love and interest are crucial to this process. There is a lot inside me that is against paying attention to myself; my personal, family and cultural history stop me from accepting and unfolding the block-resistance.

Anup: What do you mean exactly? I want to know more.

Stanya: If I use the story of Shiva going into the jungle, for me to even set off on the journey into the jungle of my inner world I need to pass the gatekeeper[4] who denies my capacity and right to do that. It requires lots of love, trust and interest to stay in this place and move beyond the gatekeeper[5]. Unfolding the block/resistance I find a wall, which was built by many generations throughout my family and national histories[6]; it's an ancestral wall with the sign, in different variations, 'You Are Not Capable or Worth It'. There is no love or interest or encouragement to go further.

Anup: So by even staying in this place you are breaking the generational pattern. This illustrates the connection between individual, family culture, nation, history, and the world.

Stanya: Yes, from this point of view the resistance is not only mine, and engagement with this issue is not only about me. It is a long process where developing awareness, through Inner Work and love, is central. When it is hard to find the love in myself for my stubbornness, because of the pain which was connected to that in my past[7], it is your acceptance and love that makes the difference. It helps me to notice what I notice: that I'm being stubborn and to open the door to that experience, rather than just fighting it, and try to be obedient. Embodying my stubbornness consciously means that I am aware and closely follow what is happening in the moment. Yes, I am challenging.

Anup: Every time we do Inner Work it's like a dance of Shiva. It's about developing the inner facilitator; detached awareness from within the experience itself. In Kundalini yoga the word for experience is Shakti. In this sense the Inner Work is the dance of Shiva and Shakti, the unity of Shiva's loving and adoring observation and Shakti's experience[8].

Stanya: Inner Work is an internal form of the dance of Shiva and Shakti. Relationships which involve love, whether it is friendship, or between teacher and student, therapist and client, are an external form of that dance. 'What makes us grow is love'[9].

Anup: That is the kind of love which is interested in the wholeness of the person and helping other person to grow. A willingness to challenge the person in the place of their personal growth from the depth of the heart. Mindell comments on this kind of loving: 'Each takes the next as a friend, partner and worthy opponent. To be a warrior means to be your true self, that is to be difficult, loving and playing tricks on your friends to help both them and yourself to awareness'[10]. That is the love of Shiva.

Nataraja, Shiva the King of Dance. from Masterworks of Asian Art, published by Thames and Hudson, 1998.

Second conversation
Shiva as Creator and Destroyer – The Eternal Dance

The story goes, that shortly before or after Shakespeare's death, when he found himself in the presence of God, he said: "I who have been so many men in vain want to be one man only, myself." The voice of God answered him out of a whirlwind: "neither am I what I am. I dreamed the world the way you dreamed your plays, dear Shakespeare. You are one of the shapes of my dreams: like me you are everything and nothing"'[11] Jorge Louis Borges

Anup: Shiva is also the creator and destroyer. In mythology, Shiva is often portrayed as stamping down violently on the head of a demon (which is symbolic of unconsciousness). This is the death aspect of Shiva which also leads to the creation of new awareness.

Stanya: Through the process of Inner Work we discover the unknown aspects of our personality; our perception of ourselves inadvertently changes. The old identity is dying[12]

and the new one is arising; this is Shiva's eternal dance of trans-formation. According to Barbara Hannah (one of Mindell's teachers) for the transformation to occur, we must love ourselves exactly as we are and also want to change[13].

Anup: As we talk about this, I'm thinking about my life-long battle with my addictions[14]. They are calling out for something in me to die. Currently I am writing a dissertation on addictions (sex/pornography). I see the unravelling of my long-term addictive behaviours as a way of expanding my everyday conscious-ness. The act of writing the dissertation is an act of love and also one of my biggest challenges.

Stanya: Yes, loving yourself and being loved for who-ever you are is fundamental to this process, as this area is heavily mined with shame and guilt, and that feeds the cycle of addictive behaviour. Yet if we dare to look inside and unravel the quality behind addiction we unleash the creativity which is locked in. I see those changes in you, and I'd love to see more of you.

Anup: The process behind my addictions feeds my voraciousness and longing, a state that I don't identify with. When I unravel this further it is a longing for the unknown. Inner Work helps me to stay aware of my longing for the unknown and live that in the moment. Staying unconscious (not noticing and unfolding my experiences) means I fall into the addiction to reach that state unconsciously, never quite reaching it.

Stanya: It's not a neat affair is it?

Anup: Fuck, no! It's a messy, painful process that I tend to hide from the world and those around me.

Stanya: By writing about it now, you are not hiding. This is a world issue that more of us need to talk about openly and with love.

Anup: I notice how the dance of creation and destruction happens in our relationship. We don't relate in only one way.

Stanya: Yes, through writing this article together; the intensity of the fights and intimacy we have had makes us feel freer to disagree and also express deep feelings with each other. Another thing which has been 'destroyed' is the belief that we as individuals are separate.

Anup: When we were struggling with writing this article, we decided to do Inner Work. By going into the essence it emerged that I was merely a channel for the universe. Nothing more, nothing less! This article just needed to be written, and in this moment we were simply the vehicle for that.

Stanya: I'm thinking of the dreams we have and how often when we talk about them together there are moments when we do not know whose dream it is.

Anup: Hindus perceive all reality as the eternal dance of Shiva and Shakti; Shiva is eternally getting to know Shakti through us. Everything we experience - love, conflicts, excitements, longings, desperations - is Shiva getting to know Shakti[15].

Stanya: From this perspective, Inner Work is simply noticing and reflecting on what's passing through us.

It's a sunny morning and we are sitting in a café in the centre of London reflecting back. We realize that the idea of us writing the article together was conceived when Anup was in Australia for the World Work seminar[16] and Stanya in London through a series of phone conversations from the streets of Sydney! The final part was written when Anup was in London and Stanya in the Czech Republic visiting her dying grandmother. The phone box became our dreaming and working space again. The physical space and time were woven with dreamtime. The events of our momentary life are reflected in this article. Being present with my grandmother in the place between life and death, we touched the two worlds; the world of time bound by a beginning and an end and the timelessness of the universe.

Eternity. Author's photo. 2002

Anup Karia

is a Student of Process Work and passionate about following his dreaming. He works as a Therapist and Group worker in London.

Stanya Studentova

life enthusiast, enjoying and studying inner and outer journeys in the world. Facilitator working with groups, individuals and families; student of Process Work.

1   'One way of understanding Inner Work is using ourselves, our individual being as a channel for awareness, in connection to the field/fields that we are part of.'
Audergon, Arlene. 2001. Inner Work Manual from *Inner Work 'Work Out'*. Supervision and training manual for seminar participants. Dec 2001. Leiston Abbey.

2   Love can be seen as an inner drive; but also as an attitude of being interested in inner development.
Audergon, Arlene and Jean-Claude Audergon. 2005. Student Intensive training. Sept 30 – Oct 5, 2005. Leiston Abbey

3   Mehta, R. and Shridevi M. (1997) Ed.3: 77. *J.Krishnamurti and Sant Kabir, A Study in Depth*. Delhi.: Motilal Banarsidass Publishers, Private ltd.

4   Gatekeeper is guarding the gateway - the boundary or an 'edge' between the known and unknown worlds, between worlds we identify as ourselves and those we don't. Edge, or in other words limits of our identity and consequently of our learning are influenced by our past experiences, culture and our privilege.

5   Self hate is one of the reasons we do not want to go inside: 'If you have love, you have curiosity for the person you work with, even if it is yourself. Love and curiosity are the basics of the Process Work.'
Audergon, Arlene and Jean Claude Audergon. 2005. Student Intensive training. Sept 30 – Oct 5,2005, Leiston Abbey

6   My grandparents and especially my parents who grew up under communist repression heard the message that they were worthless or not able to do anything in many variations. Czech is a small country, and throughout its history was overpowered and occupied by its bigger neighbours (for more than 700 hundred years). Inner resistance against the occupier, fighting and striving to preserve a coherent identity, is part of the national history. It needs to be mentioned also, that however difficult and painful this process was/is, it was also a creative process in the sense that some of the best art was born out of this striving. From one perspective any form of art is a product of Inner Work, then we can say that the cultural/artistic, and often underground, movement in Czech was also a collective act of Inner Work.

7   'Around edges extreme vulnerability occurs, then extreme love is needed.'
Audergon, Jean Claude. 2005. Basics of Process Work I. seminar Jan 28 – 29, 2005

[8] 'Shiva is inseparable from Shakti. There is no Shiva without Shakti and no Shakti without Shiva, the two are one - the absolute state of being - consciousness and bliss.'

Wikipedia The Free Encyclopaedia. Shiva. http://en.wikipedia.org/wiki/Shiva (accessed - June 08, 2006)

[9] Audergon, Jean Claude. 2005. Basics of Process Work I. seminar Jan 28 – 29, 2005

[10] Mindell, A (1993) p 166. *The Shaman's Body: A New Shamanism for transforming Health, relationships, and Community*. San Francisco. Harper Collins

[11] Borges, Jorge Luis. (2000) p. 89. *Selected Poems*. Penguin Books.

[12] 'Death is something that you live everyday with because you are dying everyday to everything that you know.'
Mehta, Rohit and Shridevi Mehta. p. 27. n 3 above

[13] Diamond J and Jones L. S. (2004)p. 36. *A Path Made by Walking*. Portland. Oregon. LaoTse Press

[14] The process oriented way of working with addictions is based on the observation that through the addictive behaviour we are trying to reach the state/quality/behaviour, which is not accessible to our everyday mind, and missing in our wholeness. In this sense behind the addictive behaviour is an intense creative and spiritual process of discovering potential we did not know existed.
Mindell, A (2000) pp. 162-172. *Dreaming While Awake: techniques for 24-hour lucid dreaming*. Charlottesville: Hampton Roads

[15] Mindell, A. (1989) pp. 63-69. *Year 1: Global Process Work*. Arkana.

[16] 'Worldwork is an experiential training seminar in conflict work and community building. The seminar provides a unique opportunity for people from all over the world to come together in a powerful forum for focusing on and working with social, environmental, and political issues using group process skills.'
Worldwork. http://www.worldwork.org/home.htm (accessed July 07, 2006)

Oregon coast, Kirsten Wassermann

Becoming Now

By Mo Ostler

Jean – Claude, I have spent so many days like this; in 'anticipation of inspiration'. This in itself has been a teaching for me. I am reminded that the essence of your teachings is in every moment; now and now and now and now.

Thank you.

Mo Ostler
is a phase two student of Process Work who lives and works in Somerset as a psychotherapist and mother.
She has always been fascinated with the synchronicities and parallel worlds in which we all live.
She discovered Process Work over nine years ago and is indebted to Jean-Claude for his eldership and teachings, and for his deep love of Process.

I have spent
The last days/months
Wondering
What
Can I write for this offering
That is me
Is not me
I feel
Empty, unable
Even as
In the considering as I walk, hoping for inspiration,
I become the sky above me
The ground upon which I walk
The sway of the grasses around me
The child screaming injustice
The mother sobbing her pain
The children's laughter in the street
The roar of the car as it passes
As it blanks the children playing
Ignores their shouts of joy
I am
The breath of the old man
As he labours on his way home
I am also
The badger curled in paralysis
Knocked dead by excited youth.
I am their blind reckless abandon
I am their thrill in the moment, their anger and blunted senses.
I walk for a while in their world
And I see that it is also mine.
I feel rich; this gift that has opened my world,
That has enabled me to see glimpses
Of the me
That is me,
But also not me
That has all this inner diversity
That does not need to reach for the impossible
Because I am the impossible
Suddenly made possible.

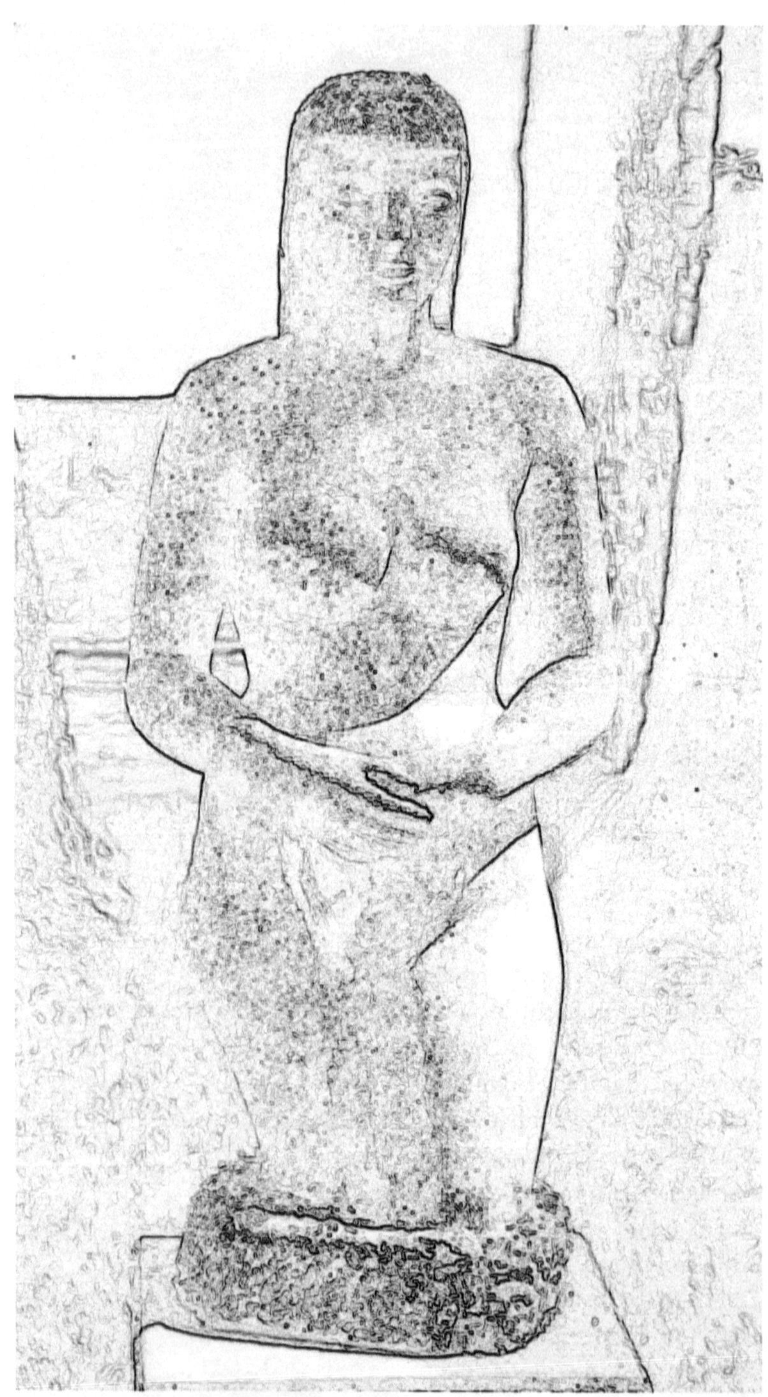

Pregnant woman, Kirsten Wassermann

The Dance of Life and Death in the Process of Abortion

By Kirsten Wassermann

'We see things not how they are, but how we are.' Jewish proverb

Introduction

From a point of view outside of our every day life we could describe experiences and confrontations with other people as a 'theatre play' or movie, where every one takes a special role. Also in a specific situation, which is for example influenced by society and history we unconsciously slip into or are chosen for a role, which becomes our perspective and creates a specific behaviour. Looking at ourselves not only as one identified person, but as a system which has different parts, these outer roles can simultaneously be seen as inner parts, which we are more or less identified with. Watching the behaviour and reactions of other people, can help us to get in contact with our own inner roles, especially the ones we don't like or try to ignore.

Not being aware of this creates a lot of pain, through polarisations and fights against each other. We try to get the power and be the winner in the situation, but hardly recognize the discomfort which comes along with it, because not only does the other person feels victimized and hurt, it is also a part of us that we ignore.

'The field only works human and wise if every role is consciously taken over and inhabited (A. Mindell). This metaskill[1] in Process Work, called 'deep democracy'[2], is to be open to all voices, feelings and behaviour in the field and in ourselves, the ones we like and dislike, the ones we want to support and also the ones we are afraid of or don't know, to create awareness for the whole situation and find the dreaming background behind it. Based on this role concept[3] developed by Arnold Mindell, I want to write about my experience of being unintentionally pregnant. Confronted with the complexity of this situation and pressured for time my partner and I decided for an abortion in the 10th week.

Starting from my unconscious identifications I used Inner Work[4] to develop different roles in the field and inside me, which helped me to accept my decision and to understand the process I went through.

This article should not be taken as either promoting the position for abortion nor the position against it, but as supporting and deepening the awareness process of women and their partners around being unintentionally pregnant. There is a lot to say about the unconscious side of getting pregnant, but I want to focus on the decision process.

The main roles in the field

Looking at the field I can identify four different main roles:
- the '**Mother**', which wants to protect the child and give her life
- the unborn '**Child**' which hardly gets a voice and is left alone
- the '**Decision Maker**': one who said 'no' and decided for an abortion
- the '**Outsider**': one who 'stays out' and passes on responsibility.

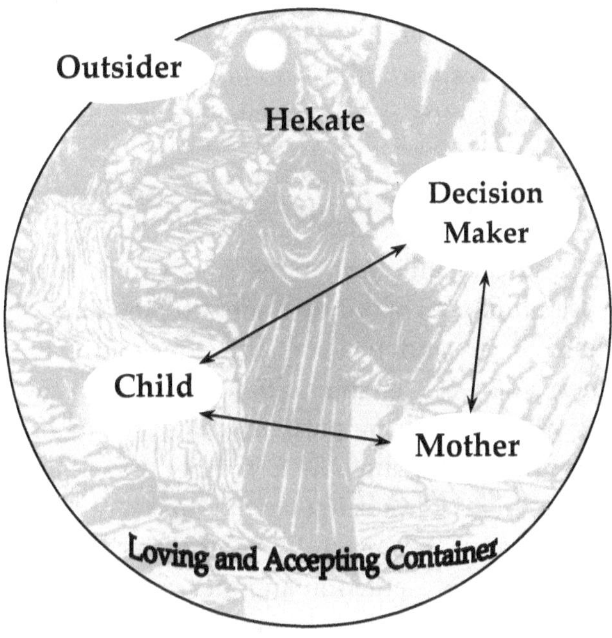

Most of the time during the decision process as to whether I would have an abortion or accept the pregnancy I was unconsciously identified with the 'Mother' and the 'Decision Maker', squeezed into the conflict of protecting life and saying 'no' to taking care of a fourth child. I was in touch with a part in me which just wanted to get out or better 'stay out' of that inner conflict, wishing for someone who takes over the decision. But the identification of being a woman, who is physically involved and connected with the developing life, stopped me from getting any distance from the conflict. And it also stopped me from giving the unborn a voice.

In this conflict I could also feel the strong collective influence. On one side there is society's law which makes abortions legal while at the same time taking the Outsider-role by passing the responsibility to the women. And on the other side there is the Christian ethic, which I have as a German protestant grown up with, which sees abortion as a sin, wanting to protect the unborn's life through moral rules and passing responsibility to God, who takes in this moment the role of the Decision Maker.

Edges against the 'Mother' and the 'Decision Maker'

Edges[5] indicate our limitations of awareness and can be seen as boundaries of our own identity, the limit of what we are able to do and believe. The edges to fully take the 'Mother' side were the difficulties in admitting my dream of having a baby with my partner whatever a child meant in that moment, not being able to mother myself and the guilt and inner critic of not being able to take care for the unborn child. The edge against fully taking the decision for the abortion was represented in an inner critic: 'You don't have the right as mother and human being to kill!' Stepping unconsciously into the identification with the Decision Maker, I felt unable to carry the child and to get along with four kids. I thought I want stay in my job and in the Process Work training, which I couldn't while having a baby. And I imagined a deep existential hole and a great fear of losing control of my life.

Even though I could develop a 'solution' at some point, inhabiting the Decision Maker was really hard and painful. Blaming my partner for his, in my view, Outsider position, blaming God that I am a woman and getting victimized from that role, the wish to be taken care of and give up responsibility kept coming back (and will be explored further).

The first step I could do, was to go into a deep inner debate with the Mother-side and the Decision Maker: An inner image I called 'Hekate' arose.

Hekate

is an archetypical figure of Greek mythology, who supports life and death. Hekate is a guardian of women in childbirth and she is the opener of the way to death. Sometimes she brings a new life into the world, sometimes she brings death. As a threefold Goddess she embodies the sky, the earth and the underworld. In a sense of knowing she takes care and brings her love through supporting the different aspects, but also stands for clear decisions.

In that state I could invite death into my life, not fighting against it, experiencing that I don't have to try to keep everything and having the ability to let go. I felt how deeply connected are both sides in taking care of life and death. On the outer level I could inhabit 'Hekate' in following experience: *The day after the abortion I made a little package with flowers and stones I collected at the beach and swam far out into the ocean, where I found a coral-reef on the bottom. With feelings of sadness and loss I placed the package and handed it over to 'mother ocean'. Swimming in the ocean made me feel mothered by myself and mothering at the same time.*

The Child

Still I felt that I missed something, which kept knocking on 'my door'. Through thoughts of 'Maybe the child would have liked to live?' I could recognize that the Child didn't get a voice at all. I also had feelings of helplessness and loneliness which I had to marginalize, being afraid of getting overtaken by them. Being not able to make a decision involving these feelings, they kept coming back. When I was able to pick them up and try to find out about them more deeply I saw that I have a need to be taken care of and give up responsibility, but it is difficult to accept this part of me, as I normally identify with strength and ability to handle everything on my own.

So this role, which I call 'child', took its place in the field as unwanted feelings and ignored needs. I was fighting against them in me as well as in my partner, attacking him for being overwhelmed and feeling helpless.

As a counsellor for pregnant women[6] and their partners I knew about the polarisation in that process, and I normally try to bring awareness to it. The men feel mostly helpless and overtaxed and at the same time being outside the decision process. They think for example that they don't have anything to do with the decision or don't want to influence the women in their decision, because it's not their 'body'. Unconsciously taking the side of the Outsider, they don't really go into the distance nor are they able to inhabit the Child's role which they unconsciously connected with through their helpless feelings. Like me, the women normally are not able to step out of their identifications, too. Squeezed into their inner conflict, they ignore feelings which disturb a 'clear decision', looking to the unborn child not taking its side or inviting it as an inner figure to support an integrated decision. But ignoring parts of yourself means they keep coming back and cause a lot of pain, e.g. feelings of guilt, putting yourself under a taboo, being in a state of loneliness and separation.

I slipped into the Child's role, when the bleeding did not stop after the abortion. I found myself in a situation of helplessness and fear of death. In this state I felt overtaxed and not able to do anything. A phone call with a midwife, who told me to go to a hospital immediately, made me aware that I would bleed to death. Suddenly I had to step back to the position of protecting myself through going to the hospital. I was in a situation of being dependant on the doctors to stop the bleeding through an operation and I felt totally left alone and afraid of not coming back from the anaesthetic. Luckily the uterus wasn't damaged and I could leave the hospital after one and a half days.

Going back to the situation of helplessness as well as to the child I said "good bye" with an Inner Work exercise[7], taking the Child as an inner figure. *I saw a picture of myself as a newborn child destined to die, surrounded with blood. My voice is not heard - no contact - all on my own - fear of death. In the depth I could see myself going into death in a place without fear, looking from a detached place of freedom, in a deep contact with life and light. Being light myself, without being embodied, no pain, no conflicts, nothing to do, I could not only accept but appreciate the part which pushed me into that place and gives me her love.*

'You didn't have it in your mind, to have a child. Your little girl was in your whole being, not only in your head. Give her birth' (L Andrews, Medicine Woman). - Who is she? - She is my heart, my love and my connection to life itself.

The Outsider

The fourth part was one of the most difficult ones to accept and get in touch with. This part often chooses the partner, who is not physically involved in the pregnancy and who is blamed for not making a decision or taking responsibility for the decision, but at the same time has no right (law, society) to be involved, too.

I tried to ignore the importance of the Outsider, through strong reactions against my partner. As I was dreaming into and interpreting his reactions as distant, disinterested behaviour, we got strongly polarized into "I take the whole responsibility" and "he none of it", not realizing the part which wanted to be seen and appreciated. Blaming my partner was much easier than to see that role as part of myself. "How can I be detached as a woman?" I asked myself at a point. "How can I not be involved in the pregnancy and the abortion, which happened to me physically? How can I be not related?"

Then in these days I had a night dream: *My partner and I both tried to survive a terrible war taking place where we stayed. Bombs were falling down in Germany destroying buildings around us. We tried to find out how to stop the war. Close friends, a couple, contacted us to tell us, that they are leaving for a vacation somewhere at the beach. I was appalled by this message, 'how could they just leave in such a situation, not caring about what´s going on?' But they left us, taking a plane south.*

Waking up I still felt the dismay. The dream came back into my mind when I was sitting outside in my sunny garden having a cup of tea. I recognized my relaxed state in this moment and got interested in the couple going on holiday in the middle of a war. Getting more and more in touch with that part of the dream without judging it, I could welcome myself getting and staying out of a difficult situation, not trying to solve it or even do anything about it, but being detached and relaxed about it. So instead of fighting and surviving I could also choose to relax and have fun. Being identified with writing the article and finishing it, I marginalized that part again which wants to get out of it, whether it's done or not. – "There it is", I thought, "right in front of me". Though there is lots more to say, I will finish here and leave for holidays on Lanzarote.

Saying "yes" to the decision I made, saying "yes" to mothering myself and taking care of my needs and at least saying "yes" to going on with life and having fun even in difficult situations, I feel a great relief.

Prospect

Why do I bring these personal experiences in?

This kind of experience happens often in a secret place, people affected are feeling alone and separated. They are blocked in these roles having difficulties integrating the different sides and getting out of the polarisation. Even if they can manage the decision through ignoring the field, their experience affects relationship strongly. Men who do not even get a chance to be involved in the decision process, stay identified with the Outsider role, sometimes with a slight feeling of guilt in the background. They are also depressed by the society's belief system, which doesn't give men a chance to engage in that process, through not being physically involved in the pregnancy. Even though we know that a pregnancy and birth of a child affects the man, society ignores the effect of an abortion. So looking only at the woman's process marginalizes the partner's role and process and also the field in which abortions happen. Therefore it's difficult to become aware of the message which tries to arise through the pregnancy and abortion experience. Hopefully this piece of work gives a wider view of the situation.

Confronting myself with these different roles and finding out about their connection and essence I feel able to be that 'loving and accepting container', which gives support to the women coming to me as counsellor to find their path through the decision process of whether they want an abortion or of being able to accept their disabled child. I don't need to judge any more, as being more able to make contact with the different roles inside me and in the field I try to make contact with where these women and their partners are identified, while at the same time supporting the other roles in the field too. Process Work calls this 'eldership'[8]. On this ground an awareness process is possible, where clients can pick up the roles which they are unconsciously identified with or which are marginalized. Through this they are often able to make a decision on a deeper conscious level, which feels right (congruent) for them and which is not only bearable, but acceptable.

Through my own process and the conflicts which came up in my partnership around the decision, I can see from this point of view, that not only the woman but also the man needs to go over their edges, and picking up these roles inside themselves as well as their partner's side, to come out of the polarisation and find their path for their partnership together. And it also helps me working with women and their partners who don't want to have a look at all these aspects, recognizing and appreciating their limits and their identification at this moment without pushing them somewhere else.

Wherever the path will lead me and my partner I want to appreciate and welcome the different roles some of which are disliked in the partnership and the field.

Thank you, Peter, for your love and the chance to go into it so deeply, and excuse me for all the accusations, reactions and fights I was identified with. And thank you for your generosity and trust which enable me to write about such an intimate process in public.

Thank you, Jean-Claude and Max, great teachers, who gave me the tools, their love and support to welcome this process as a chance for personal growth.

Who wrote that article?

Was it me **Kirsten Wassermann** ?

Dipl. Psychologist and psychotherapist, student of Process Work and single mother of three children; working at the University Hospital in Bonn, Germany, as a counsellor for women and their partners after getting a prenatal diagnosis and having to decide about a medically induced abortion; grief counselling after stillbirth and abortion.

Also, the article chooses me to be written.

[1] metaskill – see Mindell, Amy (1995) *Metaskills: the spiritual art of therapy* Tempe, Arizona.: New Falcon

[2] deep democracy – see Mindell, A (2002) *Deep Democracy of Open Forums*
Charlottesville, VA: Hampton Roads Publishing Company

[3] role concept – see Mindell, A (2000) *The Leader As Martial Artist, an Introduction to Deep Democracy*, San Francisco: Harper Collins

[4] Inner Work – see Mindell, A (1990) *Working on Yourself Alone, Inner Dreambody Work.* London: Arkana

[5] Edges – see Diamond J & Jones, L.S. (2004) *A Path made by Walking: Process Work in Practice*, Portland, Oregon: Lao Tse Press

[6] see www.praenataldiagnostik-beratung.de

[7] see n. [4]

[8] eldership – see n.[2]

Waves, Edges and Hokusai

By Margaret Godwin

Looking back over the years since the earliest heady excitements of Process Work, I realise that my life has not only changed completely but become richer, deeper, more alive. Not only alive with creative fulfilment on many levels but also I am more than ever willing to draw strength from the dark and painful areas of life and work.

Thank you Jean-Claude for the dedication to all the aspects of the work which taught us to weave and dance the patterns of the Tao and of our own individuality.

In the project at the NHS your work was stunning. We constantly witnessed that even in the dark, apparently redundant parts of life, light and change constantly renewed areas of heartbreak and tragedy. So many aspects of life to learn from, to be shaped by and you were unstinting in giving your whole energy. The rigour of your teaching stands out in all our minds. You knew how especially important it was and how privileged we were to have such an opportunity. Your work was incredible and often comes to mind while I am working with clients who experience altered and extreme states. This teaching is so useful in our cultural climate of drug use, absence of community and lack of personal meaning. You faced the waves of change, not only in following the threads of change in Process Work but in a culture that was in the midst of change, affecting the lives of your students as well as your clients. Fairly soon after you began teaching in England, you married Arlene and came to live here. I can remember the enormity of your decision. We were so pleased to have our own Diplomates and appreciate the dedication to your own work with us while dealing with and adjusting to your own life change.

In 1989 one of the most powerful events of my adult life floored me for quite some time. My son Matthew died suddenly in the night at his Art College of viral pneumonia. The shock of sudden death to myself, family, friends and those in Process Work still reverberates in my life. The extreme moments of grief are once again like waves, almost like childbirth, very difficult to describe except to say that it is like being hit by a tidal wave. I often conceptualise these moments by remembering the print by the Japanese artist Hokusai, the tiny boat enfolded by a breaking wave— terrifying until I identify with the wave as well as the boat. This is a useful analogy for me for many edges and the huge energy contained within them. The mood swings from highs to lows are the most extreme form of being out of control, like being in a nightmare.

You taught me to return to the trauma and the change held there and in that deep compassion that is without words I felt the embrace of an energy that was beyond time and place. It takes those extreme events to meet not only the essence of myself but of you Jean-Claude who worked with me. In those moments we rest in the eternal. Instead of disintegration I felt held. Every time Jean-Claude you worked with me a buoyancy returned. Working on these processes over the years, gave me the strength to continue with my life and training in an enhanced and deeper way.

Although I still miss the physical presence of Matthew, I still have an amazing, exciting relationship with him by working with night-time dreams, in fact our family share our dreams about Matthew, talking together about him and appreciating the ongoing journey with him. I have also picked up the role of painter and artist in myself, returning to painting in a renewed way as a part of him that could continue to live in the world. This is a soul expression for many creative artists in my family.

The spirit of place and time, sometimes in abstract form is the subject of a recent exhibition of my paintings and is part of the gift and expression of Matthew's life.

With many thanks for your ongoing part in this incredible journey, with many good wishes and blessings on your 60th birthday.

Margaret Godwin
is a Diplomate Process Worker and practising psychotherapist. A landscape artist, mother and grandmother she is studying painting and creativity.

Putting Down the Rock and Dancing with the Shadow

By Helen Wells

This Inner Work emerged when working with groups of mental health service users in an NHS Trust in Norwich. Groups were focused around Self Esteem and Working with the Inner Critic and participants were service users who had had a long connection with mental health services, from 3 years to 20 years.

The aim was to enable people to gain awareness of themselves, to follow and unfold their process and to connect to new patterns already happening. An essential part of the work was in exploring how people currently identify themselves, e.g. ill, mad, client, not coping, out of step with society, victim etc, and working fluidly with the emergent creative process that enables awareness that those identifications are not fixed and not the whole.

The images seem to be both mine and not mine. They emerged in my practice as an artist, in parallel with the group work. Sometimes I wonder if the images that appear in me exist in parallel worlds, waiting to appear to carry information to my awareness. They seem to hold the whole of something trying to emerge and when unfolded bring the process into my awareness.

The first is of a figure carrying its shadow. The shadow is huge and heavy, much bigger than the figure. It looks like a rock. In the rock floats another figure, a ghost of another possible way of being. The figure is worn thin from carrying this burden.

As I dream into it I imagine that this is what it is like to be a service user in the current mental health system. Carrying a heavy rock made up of a sense that one's life experiences are wrong, or pathological, that one is carrying the added burdens of stigma and marginalisation and attitudes of society toward mental illness. It also carries the repeated patterns handed down through generations. And more it carries attitudes of staff to the person identified as client, it carries internal attitudes of marginalisation of certain parts of the person. It carries feelings of guilt and failure and blame and anger and a sense that somewhere this is not right. Wow this is one heavy rock!

The second image is of a figure picking up its shadow. This time there is a life and tension between the two figures. They hold each other by the hands, feel each others weight, look as though they begin to dance. This image conveys what its like to pick up your secondary process. Primary processes are closer to our awareness, they are experiences we feel familiar with in our every day identity. Secondary processes often disturb us and are all aspects of our experience that we perceive as being 'not me', as happening to us, or we are reluctant to identify with. In the context of these groups secondary processes could be hearing voices, seeing visions, feeling anger or power or joy. I use shadow in the image to convey any part of the person that is further from their awareness in the moment. Picking up the secondary information, inhabiting it, dancing with it, unfolding it, integrating it, finding its meaning, this is a completely different way of working with what is experienced as disturbance.

The images and Inner Work connect me to the fundamental change in attitude that this work represented within the mental health system, within myself and within the group participants. Rather than using the language of illness or health we had an underlying attitude of welcoming in what disturbs us, having a loving interest in it, and further, unfolding it to find that in the disturbance is exactly what we need!

This was reflected in the feedback of the group participants about their changing perceptions of themselves:

- I have more self -knowledge and awareness.
- I'm a good person, not bad.
- I can stand up for myself and feel calmer and more creative.
- I identify myself as my ally.
- I have peeled away the last layers of hypercritical approach to self and others.
- I'm more emotional, but positively.
- This is vital to mental health care work. A lot of people's problems stem from not being allowed to move, sound freely, be expressive. This is more caring, I prefer the spiritual approach to the medical. (Collins and Wells 2006)[1]

In this small extract from the feedback the language of the comments is both assured and empowered. By welcoming and exploring their experiences they put down the rock and started to dance.

My own journey is to fully trust these 'insights' as they flash into my inner eye.

This group work, undertaken with my colleague Mick Collins, was inspired by the work of Jean-Claude and Arlene Audergon.

Helen Wells,

B.A.Hons. RAth., is an Artist, Art Psychotherapist and Phase 2 student of Process Oriented Psychology. Deeply interested in creativity and its vital contribution to a sense of meaning and wellbeing, Helen currently works in Adult Mental Health and is developing a studio space for private practice.

[1] Collins M. and Wells H. The Politics of Consciousness: Illness or Individuation. *Psychother.Politics.Int.* 4(2): 131-141(2006)

Wooden

By Kim Ward

I dedicate this poem to Jean-Claude and his teachings.

Shame is a sentiment i
ain't too familiar with
until I feel her next to me
make a demand too high
and feel that terrible low place.

Now I can look again
Can I melt?
Can I feel flesh, warmth
human again.
Stuck in those wooden clothes
sleepless nights
lonely place.

This is me too;
the Marionette
Let her walk around,
I pull her strings
she moves, and is moved by me

I am her buddy
behind, beside, around.

I move her
she and I am moved.

Pinocchio, told a lie
Lying to herself
darkness bids darkness,
The shutters come down
stay closed, tight
with no sun seeping through.

Sun-lit strings a-light her
dusty unpolished surface
a piece of furniture
to be scraped with anvil
and put on the shelve
put on display.

Who wants this hard bitter place?
No-one will buy you.

Until you come along
tie your strings
on my finger tips
and toes
I wriggle a little
in delight
of this boy - girl
who is me.

Finding the essence behind the dream figure of the Marionette is the puppet master.

This poem belongs to a long term process which appears as cycles in my life and shifts as I enter into the identity of the Bigger U or the Puppet master who turns the wooden boy-girl into a fleshy, 'real boy' to quote from the story of Pinocchio.

This shift of identity occurs in different ways as I meet with complicated, long term edge figures on the way. The growing self-love involved in this 'individuation' process, meets in me also moments of terrible self-doubts and isolation. These are some old engrained belief systems and figures which turn my body into wood; like a fine, tough barrier that separates me from the outer world or other inner dimensions. I can function from this place; walk, talk, tidy up, do many things and be many parts, but I am unable to really connect with others nor feel in touch with my deeper self. At the edge of this Bigger Me, there may appear struggles between these various parts of myself which seek air-time, this may be painful or fun, but more often than not one-sided. While connecting with the 'Bigger Me', is an ability to see and acknowledge all the parts or indeed I wonder does this puppet master create these parts too??

Kim Ward

is currently preparing for her final exams in Process Work. She works as a therapist and group facilitator. She has many years of experience working with children as a school teacher. She enjoys writing and exploring different communication styles. She identifies as a lesbian and the topic of sexual diversity continues to bemuse and fascinate her.

Being the Dalai Lama...
and other People

By Iona Fredenburgh

When you adopt the viewpoint
That all that exists within your circle of life
Is nothing but another part of you
When you come to the conclusion
There is no-one who exists who is not a part of you
You will wisely extend to yourself
An unconditional love that will be
The light of your day
The light of your night
The light that lightens up this world of ours

Peter MacKenna
Music CD: In Love

As a contribution to this anthology, I've chosen to write about a personal experience of Inner Work, and to give a glimpse of its connection to, and relevance for, our social and political world. I've described these experiences without saying much about the Inner Work tools and skills that have been used, hoping that readers who are interested will follow up that interest by reading some of the excellent books that are listed in the bibliography.

One day in a seminar in London, Jean-Claude asked us to think of someone we admired. Easy, I thought. The Dalai Lama came to mind. "Now imagine being that person", said Jean-Claude. Oh, not so easy! I felt instantly imprisoned in being someone unworthy, who dare not. First it was simply:

"It takes lifetimes of training to be such a person". Gathering momentum, religious and authoritative dream-figures from my personal history sprang into action, barring the way. "Presumptuous… the profane… stepping into the Holy of Holies." Internally, I withered under the gaze of some glaring figure who followed up the predictable "who do you think you are?" with a scathing judgement of me for presuming in this way: "Thinks she's better than she is. Hollow ambition. Ridiculous".

It's an internal 'shamer', who keeps me in check in many situations. It's active as I write, jeering and criticising, making the whole experience of writing itself a battle that seems disproportionately huge for the output. Embedded in its view-point are useful creative and editorial comments, but delivered in such a killing style that I easily become hypnotised by it. To make it an ally, I have to engage with it, wrestle with it, take its side and become it, use its strength to find out what to keep and what to throw away or change.

I'm reminded of Augusto Boal, the Brazilian originator of Theatre of the Oppressed, who said that when he first came to Europe people didn't seem to suffer anything like the kind of oppression that was familiar to him in South America. Then he discovered that we have what he described as 'a policeman in the head'; it makes external suppressors less necessary.

Arlene Audergon (2005), in her book *The War Hotel*, discusses the connections between internalised oppression and a depressed or desensitised response to atrocities in our world, whereby degrading treatment of individuals and groups is normalised. She writes:

> Freedom not only involves liberating oneself from an oppressor, but also involves getting to know that oppressor within oneself. Getting to know the internalised oppressor in

great detail is terrifying and freeing, to no longer be unconsciously imprisoned inside one's own mind and heart. Steve Biko, the South African activist, murdered by the apartheid regime said: 'The most powerful weapon in the hands of the oppressor is the mind of the oppressed.'

In my everyday life, I am aware of being very privileged: as a middle class white woman living in a relatively peaceful and prosperous English county. Privileged too in being able to study and practise awareness skills with friends, colleagues and teachers: such community with its warmth, passionate interest, encouragement and skilfulness, makes it possible to meet challenges that can be overpowering when we are isolated. And meeting the challenges in my inner dialogue is itself the Inner Work required in order to be able to use these privileges consciously for the benefit of others.

Arny Mindell (2002) talks about the inadequacy of democracy in our society if it is not rooted in an inner, deeper democracy:

> Without some form of awareness training, within the privacy of our internal autonomy, most of us behave like tyrants. When it comes to recognising different aspects of ourselves, we become dictators who simply refuse to do so. If we are strong, we ignore our shyness. If we are harmonious, we repress and/or deny our anger.
> Instead of enacting the democratic principle that the people or parts should all be represented, there is usually only one prevailing viewpoint – that of the everyday self. This 'dictatorial' viewpoint makes sure that we do not listen to the various parts of ourselves, our feelings, longings, desires, fears and powers. *Democracy – which, in principle, strives to empower all the parts – cannot work as long as it is recognised only as a blueprint for external structures.* To make democracy an inner experience, we need to engage in some form of Inner Work or inner dialogue to create a deeper democracy.

I have slowed down a moment in the story I began with. Asked to shape-shift into being the Dalai Lama, my critic attack was fast and strong, but with simple encouragement Jean-Claude enabled me to ride through it, and a moment later I was sitting with my back against the wall looking out into the room, and I'd changed. I'd shifted into experiencing – embodying - those qualities in the Dalai Lama that I admired. I had an inner spaciousness and equanimity. My perspective came from a much larger place, as if I were connected to the Source of all Being through my back, and that gave me the breadth and depth of compassionate attention that could hold all beings, all things, with a detached warmth.

What a wonderful experience. What a relief from the battle of polarities. What a great place to live from. Sustaining it really *is* the work of lifetimes. Yet the magic of Inner Work for me is this repeated discovery of quantum characteristics to our experience: that which is furthest from our identity, is at the same time right here, under our noses, under our skin.

Threads of individuation, long-term processes, weave through inner and outer experiences over the years. Transformational moments are strung like pearls, sooner or later catalysing shifts in the cellular level of our being, the community of our being, whether we will it or not.

That urge to embody these qualities I admire showed up ten years earlier, during a four day vision quest in Wales. I was pacing slowly along a woodland path, and as I passed an old tree stump, I suddenly felt sick. I'd come to believe in such signals without question over the days alone, so I stopped, retraced my steps, and asked the stump: "Why do I feel sick when I walk past you?" "Because" it silently replied "I witness with equanimity all that is, and you are not yet strong enough to do that, but it is your path to learn".

And what builds strength? Wrestling with inner tyrants, for one. And here's the weave with that other thread, turning up in a childhood dream, as lifelong issues often do. In a dream I had several times as a young girl, I am down in the corner, very little, terrified as I try to count two rows of matches, knowing that I will inevitably get it wrong. In the centre is a huge God-Devil Eye.

Recently, at a peyote ceremony where both medicine and ceremony bring certain qualities to inner awareness, my child-hood dream came to the fore. Suddenly I embodied an advocate who had previously been missing. Firmly I said to the Eye: 'She's not going to be able to count the matches right, because she used 2 or 3 of them when she burned the house down.' The Eye smiled. A spell was broken.

Inner eldership can transform tyrants and their victims into characters who have qualities to share with each other. Such a shift makes it possible to join those elders we admire, close by or far away, in facilitating similar changes in the world we share.

Iona Fredenburgh
began studying Process Work in order to train in conflict facilitation, coming from a background of political activism and psychic/shamanic work with individuals and groups. She has a private practice as well as working with teenagers with special needs, and hopes to complete her Process Work Diploma in 2007.

Boal, Augusto (1985) *Theatre of the Oppressed*. Translation by Charles McBride. New York: Theatre Communications Group.

Audergon, Arlene (2005) *The War Hotel: Psychological Dynamics in Violent Conflict*. London: Whurr/ Wiley

Mindell, Arnold (2002) *The Deep Democacy of Open Forums: Practical Steps to Conflict Prevention and Resolution for the Family, Workplace and World.* Charlottesville, Va.: Hampton Roads Publishing Co.

Mindell, Arnold (1990) *Working on Yourself Alone Inner Dreambody Work.* London: Arkana

Mindell, Arnold (1993) *The Shaman's Body: A New Shamanism for Transforming Health, Relationships and the Community.* New York: HarperCollins.

Straub, Sonja *Stalking Your Inner Critic: A Process Oriented approach to self criticism.* Manuscript in RSPOPUK Library. See www.rspopuk.com

Catching the Essence
Process Work and Yoga United

By Evelyn Figueroa

Yoga postures are the formal, physical representation of inner experiences. The word « Yoga » means to 'unite', to 'link'. It is the process of linking the different levels of experience : our physical bodies in the consensus reality plane, Dreamland[1] and the Essence level[2] clearing the way for us to become aware of the intentional field, that mysterious wave that influences us, therefore allowing us to unfold and be guided by whichever tendency is moving us.

Unfolding Disturbances... Meeting the Cobra

When I started studying Process Work, I had already trained as a Yoga teacher and so I was especially interested in bodywork and Inner Work. The daily practice of Yoga postures and breathing techniques had different positive effects on me. The Yoga programme my teacher had designed for me and which was revised every few months, brought me a sense of physical and mental balance, a higher level of awareness of my body and its sensations and also of my reactions to people and experiences. It had a calming and energizing effect and so my daily practice was like a necessary ritual.

Studying Process Work made me aware of how far I had integrated the belief system that balance and clarity were to be cultivated in all situations and that disturbances and symptoms were to be avoided or to be corrected by bringing balance and/or marginalizing them. Consequently, the Process Work idea that unfolding what was disturbing and working with our reactions to discover the information they are carrying was alluring but really scary.

As I studied Process Work and began to bring it more into my life, working on my inner and outer conflicts, or what disturbed me, on my symptoms and my moods I noticed a change in my Yoga practice. I would follow the programme my teacher had given me but sometimes, as I was doing the practice, something inside myself seemed to be pulling in another direction. Then I would focus on the experience and hear Jean Claude's voice within me, telling me "Focus on the sensory grounded information and amplify what you are feeling. Follow whatever that is. Go to the edge of the experience, unfold what is trying to happen."

I remember an experience I had while doing the cobra posture. As I got into the posture my shoulders and the opening of my upper back felt uncomfortably tight. The movement pulled and stretched the muscles around my collarbone. I focused on the tightness in the upper part of my back and could feel a wave of heat expanding downwards, towards the rest of my back. It suddenly felt like a flame, and with that came a feeling of being alive, alert, focused and ready to respond from this state to any challenge coming from the world. It was an awesome feeling and I realized I was probably experiencing the essence of a cobra when it holds itself erect.

In this experience the three levels were linked: the body, on the consensus reality level, the dreamfigure of the cobra and a more subtle level, the essence of this posture. I moved from the physical 'symptom' of tightness towards a deeper level where I was taken over by the essence of the posture.

When Heaven and Earth meet… Moving from the Essence

In my work as a Yoga teacher, I am more and more interested in creating the conditions so this link between the three levels takes place. Yoga postures help us go inwards and quieten our minds, therefore preparing us physically and mentally to catch the flirts or fleeting sensations within us. The movement then comes from our subtle tendencies.

After a couple of Yoga postures, I stand quietly and going inside myself I sense a tendency to raise my arms. I slowly move them and as I do so I feel a lightness, something moves me upwards. At the same time, my knees bend a little and I notice a tendency in the lower part of my body to move downwards. As these two tendencies move me, I notice I feel more and more stable and also light and agile. There is the feeling of being linked to Heaven and to Earth.

Conclusion

Yoga postures and Process-oriented Inner Work are a powerful combination to develop awareness of our bodies and minds and to link the three levels. When the consensus reality level, the Dreamland and the intentional field level meet, there is Yoga – Union.

Evelyn Figueroa
is a certified Process Worker and Yoga teacher living and working in Paris, France. She is especially interested in exploring the links between the body, the mind and the spiritual, and bringing awareness to how these 'levels' structure our lives and the world.

[1] Dreamland refers not only to night-time dreams but also to dreamlike signals such as symptoms and subjective experiences.

[2] The Essence level refers to pre-verbal experiences that appear as tendencies and flirts or fleeting sensations. They are subtle and are the seed from which Dreamland and consensus reality manifest.

Teachings of Jean-Claude

By Louise Warner

I used to wonder whether Don Juan was real in Carlos Castaneda books, and it is no longer important. It is the same when considering Jean-Claude Audergon. Of course my consensus reality world says he is, you see him, hear him, learn with and from him, talk with him, sit having coffee with him and greet him; he is an ordinary guy with human qualities and foibles. Yet another part is not sure and is not concerned. I just know that the 'mood' that hangs around this teacher for me has wise offerings, and supports fluidity between worlds, bringing in a sense of 'magic' into the ordinary, a truly delightful mix. In order for me to develop this, it requires practice at what Process Work calls Inner Work; this involves focusing on an issue or disturbance, tracking its unfolding both in the inner and outer experience.

This short article hopes to make more available to all the wonders of doing Inner Work and how it shifts both the depth and quality of practice. This I am still learning, and will continue to. It is also a tribute to a versatile teacher Jean-Claude Audergon.

In my early days of engaging with Process Work, I attended a seminar on Inner Work, drawn to it by the quality of heartfelt and inspiring teaching from Arlene Audergon. This time she was working with her husband Jean-Claude and despite knowing Arlene for some four years, I had never met him, yet I noticed already I had dreamed into him, as his reputation was large, a mood went with his name, one where I had intrigue, some fear and deep curiosity, not to mention a spirit of rebellion already stirring in me, connected to the role of leadership. By day three I had witnessed this man work in a way that moved me to laughter and tears all at the same time, I felt another door open inside of me and with it a trusting in the dreaming or subjective world, and a deep connection to being part of an integral system.

Prior to discovering the delights of Process Work my working life had been as a group worker and movement specialist in various capacities for 28 years. I worked as a reflective practitioner with groups and communities in community development, using a social action model for guidance. Inner Work for me used to be just a moment of pondering or something separate to my work, often taking the form of movement such as Authentic Movement. I had not discovered yet the delights of the skills and metaskills of Process Work which are needed for an awareness approach, and to track my inside information as well as the outside information and be guided in my practise by this feedback system.

Below are two diagrams representing approaches to improving practice, one from my life amidst social action and another from teachings of Process Work. I notice now I use them both, the second has fundamentally shifted the depth, quality and ease of my work.

Social Action Approach – taken from Paulo Freire's work of community development and social change.

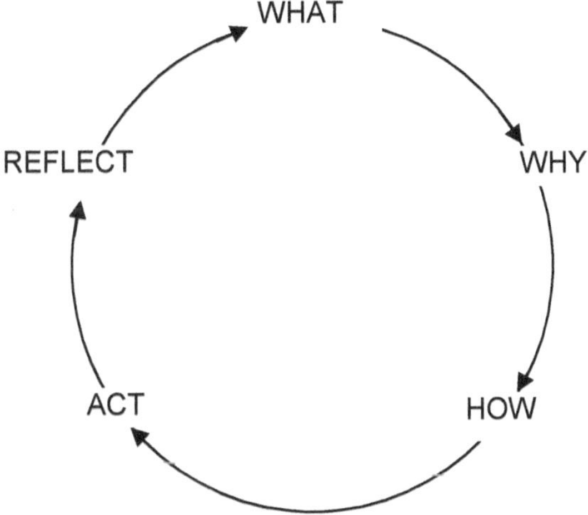

The diagram below is taken from the founder of Process Work, Arny Mindell's concept of 721 degree feedback, 360 degree inner world feedback, 360 degrees outer world feedback, the one percent allowing for the unexpected.

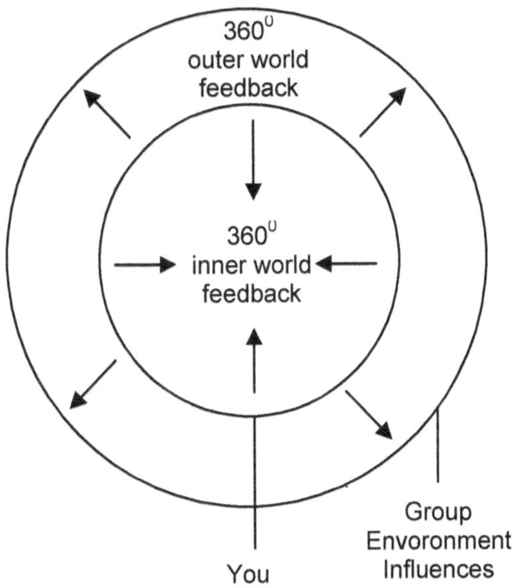

Here are a couple of sayings I have taken from teachings of Jean-Claude and how they have significantly shifted my practice as a facilitator. They have been taken from the Basics of Process Work Seminars - a series of 6 weekends in 2005.

- **'Bring an attitude of marvelling – what is happening in the moment is perfect and you are the perfect facilitator'**

Take this group I was with the other week: 18 women of differing cultures and languages, all with chronic illnesses, 5 different mother tongues, and 2 translators. My role is facilitator of a Healthy Moves session; this is using body wisdom for health awareness and potential life style changes; a complementary approach to that of the Expert Patients Programme which originated out of Stamford University and very popular throughout the UK on both the preventative and chronic illness agenda.

The room was small – a quarter of the size that I had requested - and it was run down with wonky plastic chairs. I felt the enormity of the task and found myself yearning not to be here, unconfident that I was up to the job. The group was nervous and unsure why they were there. There was a wariness of differing people and scepticism of my role – "who is this woman?" I caught myself hoping that maybe a fire alarm would go off and shift me from this place. I wanted to be 'beamed up Scotty'. I took a moment to say a little of what I was feeling, saying I was nervous, "is anyone else?" There were plenty of nods. Then I caught a robin on the window sill and I suddenly recalled the voice Jean-Claude's, *if all you remember, simply marvel at what is.* That is what I did. I took a moment of Inner Work and communicated this to the group, offering all the opportunity of doing this and simply noticing what they noticed.

I talked through scanning 360 degrees of what we could hear, see , feel, notice what part of us that is moving in the outer world, then supported us to go into our inner world, tracking what we could see, hear, feel and notice movements how ever tiny. I then took some time alone.

To my surprise the outer world shifted through my inner attitude change. This was so dramatic. I caught a glimmer of my previous fear, that part of me that is fixed, stubborn and full of doubt. I marvelled at the group, at being here together, at such a diversity of women, bodies, symptoms, various ranks and privileges. I marvelled at having a roof over our heads out of the cold winds of the Pennine hills keeping us warm and cosy (it was wet day). I marvelled at the thought that here I was, the perfect facilitator and I laughed talking this out loud to the group, and we began, talking about those parts of us that are perfect. We even dared to consider perfect pains that we suffer from, it was outrageous, and a completely new way of getting to know each other, strutting, telling stories and I felt a depth going beyond the various roles: service users, facilitator, and translator. We were 19 women of differing size, culture, age, rank and privilege, enjoying each others company. I remembered an African proverb 'the hand that rocks the cradle also rules the world'; this group held some of this quality of power, often using pains and symptoms to get there. It has continued to unfold jewel after jewel each week we have met, with laughter and tears and above all ourselves, we are the perfect group and I am the perfect facilitator. I looked at my reflective practitioner approach, and considered the reflection part I was in, noticed how Process Work Inner Work fits like a glove in this part merging these differing methods. More perfection.

- **'What is it you almost dare not…say…hear…see…feel… and then let your self do just 5% of it'**

This day was an organisational change day with a Child and Adolescent Unit, working with an eclectic team of mental health workers, advocates, consultant psychiatrists, social workers and drama/ play therapists.

We explored organisational culture, what is the 'we' of the organisation and 'what are we not'. The day developed, with an amazing amount of bonhomie and sharing but somehow I felt I was disturbed by this caring, sensitive team, and I wondered what is not acceptable to 'come out'. I noticed my edge, feeling my critic appearing, "it is just you Louise, and you can not believe everything could be so nice, it's the dark, melancholic part of you". I caught my own feedback of remembering that my critic is not always accurate, and decided to follow what I was picking up in the 'field'. There was a pause in the flow of the day, and I noticed people looking to me for where next. I had a plan, always I have a plan, I know the 'what, why and how' of this considered day and I like to know where I am going!! In the midst of the 'act' part, I was disturbed. I took a moment of Inner Work to bring more awareness to this, and noticed I was caught in a dilemma, "what is it I almost dare not say into this group?" I spoke out with some trepidation my inner thoughts, I meta-communicated, saying we could go on to looking at strengths and weakness as planned, or – "there is another thought that keeps coming back to me which is sensing something that is kept out and it makes me curious - what is it that you almost dare not say to one another?"

I was just about to look for feedback and propose some pair/small group work when it burst forth from one of the previously quiet members of the team. I caught the tone of urgency and fury and looked to the person, a guy who had been quietly semi-engaged most of the morning. He was a part time worker, the only non-white member of staff, as well as a lower paid member of the team working as a mentor. "About time, we have to stop being so bloody comfortable, so full of shit, so not really doing the work we say we do and not fully present for the children, young people and families, all the precious resources going to those that have, yet again." I caught the mood change and gave a brief weather report (this is a Process Work term meaning to name the moods and changes of the group) of this being a hot spot: a point where something hot comes up, a moment when something is touched that people often back away from and also a doorway to potential change and growth; and said that there were various responses. I mentioned about roles happening and that there was an attack around, that it was a strong accusation. I checked with everyone if it was OK to stay with this, and requested that the person say more, thanking him for speaking on such difficulty. There was momentary consensus. He spoke for a few minutes about his fury at what he saw: his colleagues simply going along with present changes, seemingly without question, being bound to outside agenda and paper work dictates, about lack of really seeing, smelling, responding to the clients, user groups, and also feeling isolated in the team. He spoke of feeling patronised by some of his colleagues, the token black guy, he spoke of lack of honesty. He finally calmed down and looked very sad speaking about his loneliness and felt lack of care towards him in this caring environment, and how part of him did not care too. There was a quiet in the room after he finished, you could hear a pin drop. I noticed and spoke out appreciation of showing himself, glad that he could say such difficult things, and bringing awareness to the learning of the role of disturbance, and how tough it is. We kept the silence, and I requested that people listen into it, noticing what is going on for them. One of the consultant psychiatrist broke down, talking of her upset at hearing him, apologising and saying she too had felt how the team was no longer so vital and creative and listening to needs of service users but taken by an outer agenda, and she had chosen to just go along with it, and do her job and not take heed.

The rest of the day was spent bringing more awareness to this, sharing feelings and being human, talking about prejudices, within the team and within a bureaucratic agenda. Many of the group were visibly touched and all felt a sense of knowing each other and themselves a bit more at the end. The dilemma of outside an agenda driving the quality of work never went away, yet the attitude and awareness around it fundamentally shifted the cultural practice to being forthright, being able to name criticism of behaviour and believing that they as a team might be a force for change.

I stood in the empty room after everyone had left, with the spirits and mood of the day buzzing around. I was fully alive in that moment, glad to be amongst trouble, valuing its disturbance and the place of deep humanity that came from it. I appreciated in that moment the teachings that had enabled me to be more fluid, to go with inner feedback and check it out and to be able to drop my linear plan and some of the outcomes for the day. I appreciated in the moment both my practice of social change from a social action approach and the layering on top Process Work 721 degree feedback in the moment. There was a relief, knowing that this needs to occur more in the voluntary and community sector I often find myself working amongst. There is a need to be less bound by outside dictates and funding driven agenda and to be more intimate and heartfelt. Life has to be about more humanity not less. I thanked my teachers in this space, Jean-Claude and Arlene Audergon for showing me another way, and another and another. Out of this day I was reminded of another 2 further teachings from Jean-Claude: "look for your edges and facilitate them" and "awareness changes conflict".

This is just a snippet of the teachings of Jean-Claude, there are many more I know and many I do not know. Above all, his honest, shape-shifting style has both role-modelled to me and been an example about the importance of Inner Work. "Know thyself" and in so doing be part of bringing deep democratic practice into the world, for all of us to walk our talk a little bit more, stepping into "being the change you want to see in the world" (Ghandi).

Louise Warner
is director of Moving for Change, a small organisation that specialises in facilitation with communities, organisations, groups and families. It places body wisdom at the core of the practice, and draws from the eclectic world of art, therapy, education and community development. Louise is a formal student of Process Work.
Louisemfc1@aol.com

Centrifugal, Stanya Studentova

Facilitation from the Inside Out

By Lane Arye

When I think of the inner world of the facilitator, I remember a time when Jean-Claude and I were in Macedonia. We had been asked by a non-governmental organisation to come train their staff as well as staff from other NGOs on how to work with ethnic tension and conflict resolution. This was one year before ethnic war broke out in Macedonia and, typically, no-one wanted to admit that there was any ethnic tension there. It seemed that they were too afraid of what might happen if that box of troubles were opened. Their neighbours - other states that had also been a part of the former Yugoslavia - had recently been through such hell that it was easy to understand and respect their fear. But the result was that we had been asked to teach about something that no one wanted to touch. And they were furious with us for bringing it up.

There was also an atmosphere among the participants (particularly among the international staff) that they knew everything already and that we had nothing to teach them. This came out as criticisms, hurtful comments, jokes, and barely audible put-downs from the back of the room.

Jean-Claude and I did our best to work with all of this, addressing it directly at times, trying to ignore it, or working with it as an atmosphere that they must suffer from. We tried our best to maintain our cool, but during the breaks we complained, comforted one another, and cried about how difficult it was. We were really suffering. I do not remember a hurtful group in all of my years of facilitating.

In spite of the pain, we did some very powerful work with them. One process that sticks in my mind happened right after we had given theory about rank unconsciousness. A group of Macedonian Albanians (the largest minority in the country) were yelling at the Macedonian Slavs (the mainstream group) about how much rank the Slavs had and how they used it to put down other ethnic groups. Of course the Macedonian Slavs were unconscious of their higher rank and denied everything. One Macedonian Albanian man in particular was furious. "You have all the rank. I have no rank at all. Nowhere in my life do I have any rank!" At that statement, all the Macedonian Albanian women in the room started to laugh. He was struck to the core. They explained the many privileges that he had in their community. From this interaction, he finally understood that it is possible to have rank and privilege without realizing it. When he spoke again to the Macedonian Slavs, he was much gentler with them, because he knew that they were probably just as unaware as he had been. They, in turn, had learned from the interaction as well, and were now open to hearing what privileges they might unconsciously enjoy. The discussion deepened and sweetened.

No matter how deep the processes went, however, the group continued to be rude, aggressive, defiant, and condescending toward us. One day during lunch, Jean-Claude and I were seriously considering taking the next plane home. We were so hurt and angry and at our wits' end. Then a change came over him. I saw him go inside for a long time and then shudder. When he finally opened his eyes, they were on fire. He told me that he was going to confront the group, get into a fight with them if need be. He would no longer tolerate being treated this way. I implored him to reconsider, begged him to either fly away with me or ride it out till the end. But he was immovable. So I braced myself for the battle, and reminded myself of the many times I had seen Jean-Claude transform blood into gold.

I don't remember exactly what happened next. I do remem-ber strong words and tears, searing honesty and exquisite vulnerability. I remember watching in awe as the entire group, including the nastiest participants, fell surely and completely in love with Jean-Claude. I saw the respect bud and grow in their eyes. I saw them learn to trust him absolutely.

The rest of the seminar was much easier, although I found myself being treated like the assistant rather than the co-facilitator. Questions were directed at Jean-Claude, people looked at him as they spoke in the group. I have to admit feeling a bit jealous. Yet I also knew that he had earned everything they gave him. His courage, his unflinching commitment to his own feelings, and his ability to make the most terrifying interaction useful to everyone, had been truly masterful. I bowed to him then, and I bow to him now.

Lane Arye, Ph.D.
co-leads a UN funded project in the Balkans working with ethnic tensions, war-related trauma, and community buil-ding. He also facilitates world-wide on diverse political and social conflicts, as well as in organisations. He is author of *Unintentional Music: Releasing Your Deepest Creativity*, Hampton Roads Publishing, Charlottesville, 2001, and co-author of 'Transforming Conflict into Community: Post-war Reconciliation in Croatia' with Arlene Audergon in *Psychotherapy and Politics International 3(2) 2005*.
Lane lives with his wife and son in the San Francisco Bay Area, where he works in private practice.

Forum, Stanya Studentova

Insider – Outsider
A Beginner's Tale of Preparing for an Open Forum

By Gina Clayton and Mike Fitter

We have found this a difficult story to tell, partly because it is a small part of a much bigger story, which is part of, contains and interrelates with other stories. We might hear a little of some, but we will never have any idea about most of them as long as we live. The telling raises the questions of what we really know, what we can really talk about. Is there anything to which we are not outsiders – even the unknown or unaware aspects of our own experience?

On one level it's all quite simple and straightforward. A highly experienced Process Worker was coming to Leeds, a city near where we live. Her friends in the city told her that areas nearby were connected with the people now known as those who carried and detonated the bombs which killed and injured so many people in London on July 7th 2005. A method in Process Work is to hold open forums: meetings for invited people or the public in general to facilitate dialogue. By comparison with many public meetings, in which particular speakers are privileged over others and the words that are said are allowed to dominate, in an open forum there is an aim for all voices to be heard, and communication that happens in other channels than just the words is attended to by the facilitators and welcomed. The two of us were inspired by the possibilities of this way of working to become students of Process Work. The aftermath of the London bombings felt to us a vital issue. The fact that the alleged bombers were British had affected us both with a sense of relief. Now there can be no further public rhetoric distancing the British people from those who commit such acts of public violence. The issue is here at home. It's our issue. Let's own it and investigate it and discover what in our society gives rise to such extreme acts. At least that was our starting position.

You might see that we were in our own states of extremity. The fact that the lead facilitator came from the USA added fuel: in our minds one of the *most* experienced facilitators from the *most* dominant nation was coming to address the *most* pressing issue using one of the *most* deeply human approaches. We were also the *newest* Process Work students in the UK. We felt the mismatch. Too much, too big, too soon, too important. Reading Arny Mindell's book *The Deep Democracy of Open Forums* relieved this initial painful though exciting state: 'if you want to do too much, you will have to depend on using your own power, and that dependence will exhaust you and make you uncertain' (2002:15). These were indeed literally matters of life and death, and a sense of their importance was appropriate, but that should not be confused with a sense of enormity about what we could do. A difficult balance to achieve – it matters hugely, and this is one small drop in the ocean. *How* we do what we do matters hugely, and yet what we can expect of what we do is in the lap of the gods. The aim is a high one, and yet in a way it is not to achieve anything. Our big aspirations and even ambitions were both vital to the process and potentially a burden upon it and upon ourselves.

Although we were both new Process Work students, neither of us were new to community events or working in a community work style. One of the things that was brand new was working to create a public event knowing that our inner thoughts and feelings were intimately relevant to it, learning to bring them in, and to unfold their relevance.

A team quickly assembled, consisting of two facilitators from outside the UK, and a group of Process Workers in the UK, some like us, as students, and some qualified practitioners. The two of us, two other students and an experienced former student lived the closest to Leeds. We became the 'footworkers' and met to process and plan. When we talk about processing, we mean finding out more about the situation by exploring the elements of it that we experience in ourselves. An uneasy feeling for instance can hold wisdom that the whole project needs.

One way we did this was by identifying some of the roles in the situation. Roles are defined as impersonal behaviour pat-terns that emerge in groups[1], also as a 'cultural rank, position or viewpoint that depends on time and place'[2]. A crucial pair of roles appeared in the group at an early stage, and although we worked with them repeatedly, they almost began to haunt us. They were the 'insider' and the 'outsider'. They came up initially in relation to the working team. The less experienced of us in Process Work identified ourselves as outsiders in relation to more experienced Process Workers. It is noticeable now that the insiders were defined by those who saw themselves as outside. We also didn't notice at the time that none of us said "I'm the insider here".

We explored roles of a 'white, middle-class, well-intentioned person', and of a 'British Muslim' going about their daily business, feeling unseen and unvalued until all this happened. In a dialogue between these two we reached a temporary resolution when breaking through the stereotypes came a demand from each side to be seen as an individual, coupled with disbelief that the other was really interested.

The insider/outside dynamic for the footworkers' group centred mainly on the question of Leeds. None of us lived there, though all of us had connections. We definitely felt like the outsiders. By contrast, the rest of the working group, who lived further away, treated us like the insiders. We pleaded not to be so regarded.

As we explored roles further in the group, we became conscious of the figure of the 'bomber'. This is also a role in the sense of being someone who does something hugely destructive and unexpected, using a power that is more than just their own (the bomb). When we considered the suicide bomber, who destroys themselves as well, we identified them as in a strange way the ultimate insider: no-one will ever be able to know fully what went through their minds. In this sense we were all trying to look into what can't be seen – no wonder we all felt like outsiders. With hindsight we missed what now seems obvious – none of us stepped into being the insider. For us as Process Work students this is a powerful though uncomfortable piece of learning. It is also connected to rank dynamics. Classically, we all tend to find is easier to see where we have lower rank, and not where we have higher[3]. Here, we projected the higher rank of the insider in a number of directions, but did not find where we were able to inhabit it for ourselves. We now see why the dynamic of insider/outsider continued to cycle so painfully for us throughout the forum process.

The footworkers' group had a predominantly commu-nity work orientation to an event of this kind, feeling an affinity with an approach that makes contacts on the ground, builds relationships, takes things at an organic pace and listens. The practical constraints upon us were that this commitment came on top of already busy lives, we had just under four months to prepare, every visit in Leeds would mean a journey for any of us, and as the lead facilitator's trip was already fixed and full of commitments, we had one evening on which the event could take place, so we needed a venue that would be available on that evening. We rapidly recognised that we were caught between an approach that we would normally feel comfortable with, and the constraints of the situation. Process Work had another perspective to provide, which was that dialogue between whoever was interested to be there on the night was valuable, so there was no need to be so concerned with some of the issues one might prioritise from a community work perspective.

Still, decisions had to be taken, first of all about where it was to take place. Fortunately, the event coincided with a peace festival in Leeds. The aims of the organisers seemed broadly in sympathy with our own, and one suggested as a possible venue a community centre serving a locality. Although not central, the centre was apparently interested in hosting events with a wider base, and might be interested. We visited with a member of the working group, a Process Work practitioner who initiated the contact with the peace festival people. It looked highly possible. We phoned to speak to the centre manager, and a conversation took place which gave us the sense that we had found the right place. After this we discovered, by looking on the Internet, that the centre had been associated with the alleged bombers, and had received intense press coverage in the immediate after-math. Did that make the idea of holding the forum there right or not? Two of us went to an evening event there on the manager's invitation, concerning civil liberties and the need to connect between diverse communities. We felt we were really connecting with a local agenda, that this was timely and right.

Then things got stickier. Communication with the centre manager became more difficult to achieve. From a sense that we might be working together, suddenly we had a sense that we were customers whose needs the centre desired to meet because they practised hospitality. The manager had initially thought that we might meet a need for mediators on a particular occasion, but that need became filled, and that changed the dialogue. We became acutely aware of the pressures upon her, the trauma that the centre had been through, and our initial ignorance of this.

The team in discussion had identified two options for a venue:

1. To work in partnership with a local community centre who would become the primary host. An implication of that option was that hosts would involve their local community and we would ensure the advertising reached a wider audience too.

2. To use a central venue not affiliated to any particular locality. We recognised that neutrality would not be achieved by this as any venue has associations which are more congenial to some people than others (e.g. a pub or a university). Any choice would favour some likely attenders and discourage others. In the background, at least for the footworkers' group, was probably a wish to have the event accessible to people who would not travel into the city centre to an evening meeting, and this would weigh against a central venue.

It followed that we excluded the option of booking a local community centre as a venue without working closely with them.

Now it began to look as though we were going to be using the centre as a venue only or not at all. Was that the right thing to do? We earnestly sought dialogue with the centre. Time was going on. Printed publicity was needed. It was the collective view of the working group that we should not just use a local centre as a venue without partnership. In retrospect, the signals we were getting were that that was not the view of the centre itself. However, at the time we did not know how to interpret the difficulty of getting contact. Did the silence mean we were unwelcome? Something was wrong? We were desperate for direct dialogue, though now we realise that we were fixing on one channel of communication. The centre's non-communication was a signal too. As the footworkers we were in agonies of uncertainty. Having made the contacts with the centre, and guided by our ideas about community work, we felt strongly defensive of the centre from invasion by simply being used by us. We seemed increasingly driven against ourselves, going in a direction we did not feel right to go. Again with hindsight, this was our agenda, not the centre's; our fixed identity was causing us grief: "we are the sort of people who do not impose upon local communities, particularly those traumatised by association with the London bombings". Now here we were, invading and imposing like crazy, in order to get the welcome we had not yet thought to offer. Still we were struggling to be in, still not recognising our own inside-ness.

When finally two of us spent several hours in the centre, getting the dialogue we had so desperately sought, we discovered that the centre was indeed happy to be a venue, but was overloaded in many ways, and though they liked what we were doing and would have been happy to offer more in the way of partnership, they simply could not. They were over-stretched. This visit was followed by a range of emotions for us: the relief of contact, gratitude at the centre's generosity on that day, triumph that we had at last talked fully with the centre about our aspirations and heard their views, shame that we had indeed imposed on those who already had too much to deal with, and embarrassment at having been so caught in our own ideas.

Again in retrospect, and following exploration in the context of our studies, we realised that in the preparation for the forum we were ruled by two predominant sets of thoughts-feelings: fear of trampling on the local community and the work already done there, and a feeling of being outsiders to the local community, good-hearted and so wanting to be welcomed, but not yet feeling welcome. We did not connect the encouragement of the facilitators to feel well about what we were doing with the need to step into the role of the welcomer, the inviter, the insider. We did not become the 'host', welcoming the experience and achievements of the many, and this remained a ghost, or unoccupied role.

A few days before the forum we met at last as a full team face to face, with some other people who were also interested, to train for the forum event. It was an enormous pleasure to meet together having worked remotely for these months, to be face to face with the team of four facilitators and to appreciate the depth of their preparation and experience. We held a mock forum, and did some work to connect ourselves with some of the deeper, communal waves that underlay the inspiration for the event.

When the forum finally happened, it was well attended, and many people were buzzing with the excitement of being able to really exchange thoughts and feelings in a public event. There were powerful and personal moments of real dialogue, moments of being heard and not being heard. It started, however, with the big question, and this from a speaker we had asked to say something from his own perspective: *"What the fuck are we doing here?"* It was a shock and it was not a shock. It was the question we had struggled with for months. It was also a relief in a strange way that it was made so real. And then we were able to say to each other – well yes – what *are* we doing here? There must be a reason. This is not only an attack, it's also a profound question. We have an international team of facilitators, we have people attending from all over Leeds and several from further afield. Why have we come to this place? And though there were no doubt many answers, one that emerged was "because it's all our concern". Much was said about the pride of the area, how people had stuck together, how it had developed thanks to the energy and commitment of local people, how it engendered strong loyalties. But also, people from further afield wanted to come and share their questions. As we had felt in the beginning, it's *all* our concern. The people of the area have done their part, and there is a place and a need for the wider world to come and join in the debate.

As new Process Work students we had something of a baptism of fire into the world of open forums – not through the forum itself, but in the preparation stage. Writing this has been another stage in learning about the process, and it feels as though there is more to go. We found in ourselves the roles that were present in the situation, and this helped us to be really engaged in all levels of the event. We began to learn what it means to process in ourselves the dynamics that are in the issue we are dealing with. We didn't see the things that were closest to us, the most under our noses. Afterwards some of us met to gather together the learning that had come out of the forum. There was a lot of it. We listed the things we would do the same another time and things we would do differently. In 'the same' list we put 'take niggles seriously and share them'. In the 'differently' list we put 'act even more on fears and niggles and share them even more and when we did not do that, be curious'. We realise that those fears that kept us frozen contained far more information than we had imagined.

And now we are beginning to realise that the perceptual shift is to *really* recognise the field nature of roles we experience, they don't belong to us personally. We each pick up a part in the cosmic drama, whether we know it or not. In this sense, there are no insiders and no outsiders, only moments of being swept along, moments of awareness, and moments in which we are willing to step fluidly into field roles so that they become occupied.

Gina Clayton and Mike Fitter
are training simultaneously in Process Work and Buddhist ministry. They are married to each other.

Gina has practised as a lawyer and is the author of the 'Textbook on Immigration and Asylum Law', Oxford University Press, 2006, 2nd edition.

Mike is an organisational psychologist, working mainly in the health service. He is also involved in community mediation.

---

[1]   www.maxfacilitation.net

[2]   Mindell, A. *Sitting in the Fire* (1995) p. 42, Portland, Oregon: Lao Tse Press

[3]   e.g. Mindell, A. above p.50

Inner Work:
A Personal Exposition and
Appreciation

By Rosamund Hoskins

Process Work *is* Inner Work, with applications as many and varied as there are people who practise it. Limitations of how *far in* and how *far out* the applications go are marked only by inner and outer rules or beliefs along with the systems that keep these in place.

There are a few guiding principles. I am a microcosm of the world I inhabit and my inner reality reflects the play and inter-play of outer life. I am not divorced from what I perceive as 'Other', whether it be a tree, an atmosphere, a person, an attitude: the 'Other' is always an aspect of myself. The art of Inner Work to pierce the common state of unawareness requires the metaskills of deep democracy, a non-exclusive invitation to be fully present, welcoming the unwelcome and unexpected as much as their opposites. Working deeply on myself, I work deeply on, and in, the world.

Three Acts of Inner-*Opera* - Far Out In the Middle of Things

One
Stepping into the Unknown in Leeds (1995/6), Jean-Claude, in the role of facilitator, paused to check an inner calling for

attention: something had touched him from his personal history. Unravelling it with ease and fluidity in the middle, his inside work came out again, full circle, to support the outer process. This was a revelation. A painful moment in the past, revisited and 'inner-worked', became a sensitive and powerful force, an act of generosity to others. Silent and in secret, I was inspired.

Two

Within a circle of creative noise in Norwich (1998?), Jean-Claude's ears heard something silenced. There was an invitation offered, once, twice, perhaps three times, to which, at last, I could respond. I found myself drawn out with patience, held in detachment, met full-far-out-and-in the middle of everything on a journey which continues still.

Three

A story begins walking in the mountains with Jean-Claude and a butterfly. Later in London, the Inner-Work Smith remembers his anvil. Strength and Delicacy in practice: a far-out path in process.

Rosamund Hoskins

is an Alexander Technique teacher. She is also a piano teacher and performer. She has been involved with Process Work for more than 10 years and continues to learn from and be inspired by its depth and potential.

butterfly and anvil, Rosamund Hoskins

To be or not to be – a Superposition?

By Clare Hill

When reflecting on a contribution to a book for Jean-Claude on the relationship between Inner Work and the world, I reflected on my recent experiences with body symptoms. I discovered that despite appearances, the post-operative state abounds with proprioceptive[1] awareness, and that facing life-threatening diseases is a wonderful opportunity to review the nature of existence. The following is an attempt to describe these states.

When I walk on a hill, the wind blowing in my hair, not too strong, not too mild, but enough for me to feel myself almost flying, arms out, gravity defied, then do I begin to reconnect to my bird nature. I remember that I don't need to identify only with my parochial self, but to remember that I too am eagle, can fly above, can swoop below, can soar upon the next updraft, and can be taken rather than take. When both I and eagle are, then in that moment I/we are smeared across the universe.

Christmas Eve, Friday 24 December 2004.

I had decided to nip into the surgery to get the pain in my belly checked. The sensation wasn't particularly onerous – about the same as someone placing a bit of pressure on your wrist. It had been there since the previous weekend, and more importantly it wasn't moving, wasn't changing. I had also noticed that I had developed – ever so slightly - a protective stoop. Neither of these was a good sign. I rang the surgery, and got an appointment for 10.15 am.

I had half of the bedrooms ready for the arrival later that day of assorted children and grandchildren. I began to measure out the ingredients for our 'special mince pie pastry'. My son and I love this recipe, the pastry rich with ground almonds, and I measured out three times the usual amount – plenty for Christmas and some to freeze for New Year. Suddenly I noticed the time – I left the ingredients in the bowl, and jumped into the car.

It was a pot luck open clinic, and a doctor called out my name – a tall man of serious but gentle disposition. I told him about the pain, the stoop, and he asked me to get upon the trolley. He began to explore my belly, gently at first as I flinched, but as the body did its miraculous adjustment to the pain, his fingers probed more deeply, more thoroughly. "Well", he said, "let's see if anyone is in the Borders General Hospital on Christmas Eve. You either have something wrong with your aorta, or there is something lying on top of your aorta." A phone call established that there were staff around, and my G.P. gave me a hand-written letter for A&E. I went back home to my husband, Conor. "I have to go into the BGH to see what's going on. Will you come with me? I'll take an overnight bag just in case."

A sweet house doctor examined me. By then it was closer to 1 p.m., and a cardiac consultant appeared. He was probably of Eastern origin, maybe China or Taiwan, and he carefully felt my abdomen. He asked the young apprentice what she thought, and she made an attempt at a diagnosis. He carefully and emphatically overruled her: "Feel this here, and notice her breathing there…" he seemed certain that my aorta was OK, more certain than she. I needed a scan of my belly, but overheard phone calls saying the consultant was about twenty minutes drive away. Eventually, I was wheeled into a room. A new consultant was there, plus my Eastern acquaintance of earlier. He seemed as curious as me as to what was going on! The usual gel was smeared on my belly and then the sonic device rolled over the area. Gradually a hazy grey image appeared on the screen beside us. I remember an exchange of conversation about a protruding something or other. I have often wondered what that was, and whether it explains why my midriff is so much more out there than other people's.

And then, sleepy now, half a day of doing nothing but lying on a trolley, I was suddenly aware they were talking about that bit there on the screen, an even more hazy part surrounding my colon. "That's it", they said with excitement, "nothing to do with the aorta." I needed an MRI scan to determine exactly what this hazy bit was, and was wheeled into nuclear medicine. A nurse inserted a tube into my wrist, and some metallic substance which would make the imaging clearer, warning me of possible nausea. I was pushed into a large metallic doughnut ring as far as my belly, and then a plate lowered to above the area they wanted to examine. Strange noises ensued, and then it was over. A long wait. I could hear discussions going on behind the partition. Male voices. Eventually I was wheeled into the corridor. The radiologist who had done the scan approached me, accompanied by a stranger, but his demeanour told me he was a consultant too.

"We think you have a cancer", the stranger said, "and we would like to operate". I vaguely remember some conversation, the gist of which was where's my husband, he needs to be here for this. Conor, last seen in A&E, approached us, carrying my handbag. "We want to operate as soon as possible". "But it's Christmas Eve – I have a houseful of guests arriving at 5 pm. and I still haven't made my mince pies!" "It needs to be done, preferably at 10 am. tomorrow morning". "Couldn't I go home, do Christmas and come in on Boxing Day?" "You could but you couldn't eat anything – it is too dangerous. You have an obstruction to your colon and it's critical. If you carry on, your body will start to vomit all the time."

When I heard that I felt my spirit give in – to dash home and do all that work for tomorrow, for Christmas, and not to be able to join in – was it worth it? Possibly not. I heard Conor reassure me that they could manage. Suddenly this camel dissolved through the eye of the needle and reappeared on the other side, into a parallel reality. It was as if I suddenly jumped off one set of railway tracks and landed on another. Conor and I looked at each other and we knew – more or less – what was coming. I was wheeled up to Ward 8. By now it must have been about 4.30 pm.

The anaesthetist arrived to talk me through the procedure, and to check on any allergies, etc. She warned that if any babies planned to arrive and needed medical interventions on Christmas morning, the operation would be postponed till later that day. The consultant went on emphatically, explaining that a diagnosis of cancer was scary, but that she was a living example of life after cancer. She had had it a few years before and was leading a full life. I noted her encouragement, but somehow a slightly removed position in me had kicked in....I was a little apprehensive about what was to come, but life and death? They seemed surreal, as if I was touching that superposition which contained all realities but identified with none. Yet that state proved to be fleeting…

I heard fast footsteps down the corridor, and knew immediately the fiery horse nature of my daughter was coming towards me. She cantered into the room, her mane of hair streaming, swathed in a winter coat and shawl, tears in her eyes. "Oh, Mum…" We hugged, silently, crying together. Five minutes later, having parked his car, my son, a slower and more cautious soul, came in, moved up to my bed, and slowly leant down for a hug. "Golly gosh!"

The four of us laughed and cried together, and began to plan how they would do Christmas instead of me. "You'll find that the Good Housekeeping Cookery Year book will give you all the details about how to roast the turkey. The stuffing's already prepared"….gradually we all made our various preparations for the day ahead. The anaesthetist had suggested they phone in at 1 pm. to see if I was OK, and to visit me about 5 pm., after I had come round properly.

Eventually they left. Before we parted, Conor handed me a beautifully illustrated book of Rumi's verses called 'Hidden Music'. "This was in the car, waiting to be wrapped up", he said, "So you might as well have it now. Happy Christmas!" After they had gone, I began to prepare myself, and thought that the book may show the way. I opened it randomly, only to come face to face with a poem about death. I snapped the book shut – so much for superpositions…suddenly the possibility of death felt close and I shied away from it.

The night staff gave me a pill 'to ensure a good night's sleep'. The next thing I knew it was 8 am. on Christmas Day and they were giving me my premed. Reality and time slipped. I recall entering the theatre, with a large circular overhead light, and a round farmer's wife of a theatre sister, all curves, pink cheeks, mop hat covering her head and voluminous aprons, who asked me to sit round and face her as they gave me the epidural. I heard the anaesthetist's voice of the day before, and leant my cheek against the round woman's shoulder as I felt something being inserted into my rounded back. The last thing I recall is sobbing strong tears into her uniform, crying for me.

I became aware of being flung from side to side, like the drum of a washing machine crashing against its case. Intense, powerful, relentless. Bang, bang, bang. My attention was deep inside myself. What was happening? Then warmth began to emanate over my whole body, deeply relaxing…

"Hello", said a smiling face quietly in a darkened room, "You're back with us in the ITU. Everything's gone beautyfully. You had the shivers when as you came round, but we put a warm blanket around you and you soon fell asleep again"….

Hazy images began to come into sharper focus. Someone at the bottom of my bed, speaking to me. I opened my eyes wider – Conor, Aaron and Gemma! Slowly my consciousness awoke, and I saw the joy and relief in their faces. I smiled, held out a hand: "Happy Christmas!" "Happy Christmas, Mum! How are you feeling?" They regaled me with how they had done the day, cooked everything to a tee, if later than usual, and even brought a bag of presents in for me. "Not just yet, loves, I couldn't enjoy them. Keep them till I come home." We were quiet together, in the quiet room and its dim light, but the pleasure at being with one another was acute. After a short while I noticed how weak I felt. "Can you put your hands on me and give me some energy?" I lay back and gratefully received the loving kindness that emanated through their arms. We talked some more, and then – somewhat to my surprise – I told them I was tired and that they should go home now. Later Conor told me they were only there for about half an hour – it felt like a very long time.

"Would I like a bed bath?" Why not? – I was sweaty and dishevelled and I had never had one before.

A nurse prepared a huge bowl of warm water, and gently began to wipe my face. Instantly my whole body became alive, an exquisite and unexpected response so soon after an anaesthetic. Was this really happening? Surely you would be sluggish now, Clare, your senses dulled? As she slowly and carefully made her way down my whole body, each place she touched became aware of itself, as if the nerve endings were being renewed; not renewed with the usual vague sensation of skin or self, but rather a heightened awareness, a deep appreciation of my body, a glorious sense of being present to myself, of being alive. And then more sleep….

I became aware of a strange sensation underneath me. I focused on the point where my skin made contact with the bed. It was as if certain, distinct parts of my body were lying on top of masses of tiny caterpillars which were moving very slowly. as I imagining this? I concentrated further. No the sensations were still there. "Nurse, I think my bed is moving!" "Don't worry, it's a special mattress full of individual cells which shift position so that you don't get bed sores"…

"Would you like a sip of water?" The nectar awoke the cells within my mouth, my throat, ran down my oesophagus, like rain drops running down a dusty window, creating a clearer perspective. Cool, refreshing, so extraordinarily present….

All of these bodily experiences made me acutely aware of LIFE. I had expected to feel half dead, or ill, but I only felt a surge of life, a desire to be on this planet, to get well again. My attention was at a microcosmic level, and bursting with vitality.

Somehow two days passed, a mixture of acute, joyous, proprioceptive sensibility and a semi-conscious blur, as if my normal awareness faculty had abandoned my brain and lodged in my body. I guess my cognitive processes were knocked out by the anaesthetic and morphine drip, and a more primeval awareness had taken over. Only this so called primitive state surpassed most of the awareness states that I have been consciously working at since I was 18 years old. They were simple and exquisite.

I was moved back to Ward 8. Despite only having one third of my colon remaining, now attached to my small intestines, after a further 5 days there was the joy of miniscule amounts of solid food again, followed by my and my consultant's anxiety about whether or not it would make its way out. And, most importantly, would it hurt? Late on New Year's Eve I was agitated and couldn't sleep. I began to focus down into the sensations I was experiencing, tiny little movements all around my sacrum, within my pelvic area. Suddenly it occurred to me that this just may be the beginnings of a bowel movement – tiny movements for tiny amounts of waste. I heaved my beached whale of a body out of bed and padded through to the loos, only to emerge triumphantly ten minutes later. It was 11.55 pm. and one of the best Hogmanays[2] ever!

Eventually I was allowed to go home. The drive was full of joy at being able to breathe fresh air, to see the wind in the trees, the hills, the sky.

And then began a strange time – getting stronger, slowly eating more, tummy muscles healing, and not knowing the results of my biopsies. The lymph gland next to the obstruction was enlarged, which was apparently either because it was also cancerous or because it had been working hard to deal with the cancer. The four public holidays meant I would have to wait longer than usual for results. I noticed that a detached state came into being: I was living in no-man's land, an imminent present, un-known future, nothing certain, nothing predictable. A strange state of enjoying everything and also taking nothing for granted. Of experiencing masses yet also not identifying too much with what I was feeling. I was simultaneously intensely alive and very detached. I could choose whatever I wanted (as long as it wasn't too physical!) and did not much mind what I chose. Meaning and meaninglessness ceased to be of such importance. The notion of right or wrong was impotent.

I remembered reading about Schrödinger's[3] cat, and it suddenly made more sense to me. Like me and my eagle self when walking, in the state of 'waiting for results' I was both alive and dead. I had had cancer of the colon, most of which was now removed. Would I have secondaries in the lymphatic system? Would I die? I noticed that I didn't know, nor could I know, but that somehow this longer time period between sending off the specimens and getting the results meant that the universe could organise itself into the 'right' way. But what would the right way be?

I eventually got impatient and phoned my consultant's secretary. He was on holiday. The results had come through, though. Surely someone must be there in his place? She would see what she could do. Forty eight hours later the phone rang. "Hello, it's the registrar here." I remembered the doctor well, a nice man. "I have your results." He began talking about good news. I could hardly make any sense of what he was saying to me. I kept listening and felt totally confused. Some two minutes later, I said "You mean not only do I not have cancer in the lymphatic system but that I never had cancer at all?" I was incredulous. "Yes, just that: you had an abscess in a diverti-culum, a protruding sac in your transverse colon. It would have needed surgery anyway, it was pretty serious, but not cancer."

A different set of train tracks appeared in front of me.
The cat lived.

Schrödinger's cat[4]:

In 1935 Schrödinger published an essay describing the conceptual problems in QM1. A brief paragraph in this essay described the cat paradox.

'One can even set up quite ridiculous cases. A cat is penned up in a steel chamber, along with the following diabolical device (which must be secured against direct interference by the cat): in a Geiger counter there is a tiny bit of radioactive substance, so small that perhaps in the course of one hour one of the atoms decays, but also, with equal probability, perhaps none; if it happens, the counter tube discharges and through a relay releases a hammer which shatters a small flask of hydrocyanic acid. If one has left this entire system to itself for an hour, one would say that the cat still lives if meanwhile no atom has decayed. The first atomic decay would have poisoned it. The Psi function for the entire system would express this by having in it the living and the dead cat (pardon the expression) mixed or smeared out in equal parts.

It is typical of these cases that an indeterminacy originally restricted to the atomic domain becomes transformed into macroscopic indeterminacy, which can then be resolved by direct observation. That prevents us from so naively accepting as valid a ``blurred model'' for representing reality. In itself it would not embody anything unclear or contradictory. There is a difference between a shaky or out-of-focus photograph and a snapshot of clouds and fog banks.

We know that superposition of possible outcomes must exist simultaneously at a microscopic level because we can observe interference effects from these. We know (at least most of us know) that the cat in the box is dead, alive or dying and not in a smeared out state between the alternatives. When and how does the model of many microscopic possibilities resolve itself into a particular macroscopic state? When and how does the fog bank of microscopic possibilities transform itself to the blurred picture we have of a definite macroscopic state. That is the measurement problem and Schrödinger's cat is a simple and elegant explanation of that problem.

From: Paul Budnik *paul@mtnmath.com*

Clare Hill

lives in Edinburgh and the Scottish Borders. She is married to Conor McKenna, a fellow Process Worker, and together they work both in the UK and on the Continent. Clare is currently the Student Coordinator in RSPOPUK.

[1]   Proprioception is a term used to describe the body's sense of itself, the experience of a bodily state, at a deep and often cellular level.

[2]   Hogmanay is the Scottish term for New Year's Eve, also known as Auld Year's Night.

[3]   See extract explaining Schrödinger's hypothesis at the end of the chapter.

[4]   E. Schrödinger, ``Die gegenwartige Situation in der Quanten-mechanik," *Naturwissenschaftern*. 23 : pp. 807-812; 823-823, 844-849. (1935). English translation: John D. Trimmer, *Proceedings of the American Philosophical Society*, 124, 323-38 (1980), Reprinted in *Quantum Theory and Measurement*, p 152 (1983).

I can do it, Kirsten Wassermann

A Lesson for the Inner Critic

By Sara Jones

A few years ago, while preparing for exams in Process Work theory and struggling with my inner critic, I had the following amazing dream which has become the guide for all my work since…..

I am working with a client in the middle of a supervision seminar and really struggling, but getting help from peers. However, my father keeps getting in the way by talking to me and making comments. He then tries to draw Jean-Claude into an alliance with him by talking about me in a belittling and shaming way. Jean-Claude says nothing but later in the seminar, he hands my father a letter he has written which goes into detail about my father's limitations of knowledge in psychology - he says my father's understanding is equivalent to out-dated theories from the 1940s, and explains in detail why my father's input is out-of-date, theoretically poor, lacks understanding of process philosophy and is unhelpful. Furthermore his personal comments about me were inappropriate and impolite. Finally, his presence is not welcome at the seminar because his critical, non-curious attitude is distracting and unhelpful to everyone. Jean-Claude shows my father an example of the modern equipment we use in Process Work: it is a Cathode Ray Tube, which is a device used in electronics for visually monitoring feedback signals! The letter contains many suggestions to facilitate my father's learning.

This dream has remained with me as a secure touchstone, a new principle for fathering my development as a Process Work practitioner. My inner critics are learning new skills and metaskills and evolving from being power-hungry and goal-oriented to being aware, accurate and signal-oriented. My deepest gratitude to you, Jean-Claude, for all your teaching and modelling of accuracy and for bringing the awesome world of fields and signals into each moment.

Sara Jones is a pen name.

Multiple Maps:
The Inner World of the Facilitator and the Outer World of the Organisation

By Andy Smith

A huge part of the inspiration to write this comes from my appreciation of Jean-Claude Audergon for reminding me time and time again about the value of Inner Work and of how the circumstances that seem most difficult or intractable are the right ones for me and for the organisation, group or person with whom I'm working.

In the Process Work paradigm, the facilitator plays a part in the system not as a detached entity above the situation or beyond it and not just linked in but coupled inevitably together with it. This viewpoint has led to the development of methods in Process Work that focus on the facilitator's awareness of what is happening to them; believing in that and then finding ways to make that awareness accessible to others (whether an individual, couple, family or organisation) so that this new information can be processed to enrich the picture of what is happening and how to support that to happen more. Jean-Claude Audergon describes...

> The original focus of Process Work was to research connecting patterns between dreams, body symptoms and signals. The body was viewed as a channel for potentially creative polarities of the individual seeking awareness. With communication theories and a systems perspective, Process

Work began perceiving and unfolding this dreaming pattern in relationships and communities in conflict.[1]

In my work with organisations I have learnt that what happens in the inner world of the facilitator is part of what is happening in the organisation they are working in and it is necessary to 'bring oneself in' as a facilitator. By 'bringing oneself in' I mean not just coming in as an empathetic or congruent person but to also bring in more freely the sometimes less obvious parts of oneself, knowing at some level that the information there will be needed by the organisation. This demands an increased awareness in the facilitator about their limits, what they feel they can bring in and what they cannot or what they think might be forbidden. Personal Inner Work becomes a crucial and often liberating requirement as it helps to bring awareness to these limits and the edges within the system.

I find it useful to also remember that each system contains only so many possibilities within it (these may be more or less unpredictable). For example, if we imagine two streams running through farmland, then each of these can be defined as a system but each particular ecosystem has particular possible futures. These futures are dependent on the history of the stream, the particular geophysical make-up, the rock beneath, the rocks within it, the current living beings that populate it and what is running off the land into the stream. Systems constellate these limits of possibility so that what is possible within one system is not possible within another.[2]

Illusions of detachment are sometimes just a way of being separate

In different ways, many commentators and researchers have explored the contrasting myth or ideal of the detached facilitator. In individual therapy, Carl Rogers, (whose person-centred school of therapy has been very influential in social work and health settings in the U.K.) emphasised the core conditions for the relationship between the therapist and the client – this contrasts with the rather detached (or removed) analytical therapist evident in classic psychoanalysis.

The relationship between the facilitator or therapist and the person is seen as essential to the success of any work that requires a level of authenticity and honesty on the part of the facilitator in order for it to be useful. For example, in the film Good Will Hunting[3] the hero of the piece, Will Hunting, meets three therapists, two of whom he 'gets the better of', partly because they are not fully engaged with him person to person. Instead they attempt (unsuccessfully) to keep a detached observer overview whilst trying to stop other parts of who they are from entering the mix. This leads to a challenge from Will, the hero of the story and reactions to then blame him, the client, for the problem. His third therapist begins to develop a 'right relationship'[4] with him when he doesn't hide his own weaknesses and difficulties, shows his own limits and difficulties: bringing himself in.

Excellent as are the foundations of the person-centred approach, like unconditional positive regard and so on, there are limitations too. Having unconditional positive regard for a person's worth is useful but is limited if it only sees the primary part of the person, and will not bring awareness to what is secondary in either party, neither will there be a process of dialogue and exploration between these parts. Arlene Audergon has explained it is as 'inadequate' to consider oneself out-side the dynamics of the system one is facilitating within:

> It is useful to strive to be aware of how your own personal and collective history and your own limits of perception involve you in the system, so that you can facilitate the

interaction of all the parts, including the one you may be inhabiting[5]

Mapping the internal and external worlds

Mary Midgley[6] is one of an increasing number of writers who outline the post-enlightenment tendency to particularise and dismantle into parts as if people are machines and facts and not complex wholes in a multi-layered system, requiring multiple maps in order for true 'sense' to be made. She suggests that we need these multiple maps because in order to see the whole we would ideally be beyond that, but of course we can't be because we are part of it. The idea that reality is multilayered and can be best understood through multiple maps or lenses reminds us that it's useful to not focus down on one thing especially when we are trying to get a sense of the complexities of things. In a lineage of thought that might include Gregory Bateson's[7] exploration of the idea that the map is not the territory, Arlene Audergon[8] also reflects on this process by reminding us of the importance of looking both at what emerges from inside a system and also what influences from outside the system and how this leads to the realisation that we can choose (with awareness) the level we view the system from.

As organisational consultants then we might map not only the system and patterns within an organisation but also would look at the system and patterns coming up in the facilitator and see these as being interrelated and then coupled. Maturana and Valera[9] have a term to describe the relationship between an organism and the environment which they call 'structural coupling'. In short this describes how development and change within one is coupled to that within another. Organisms don't evolve along some predestined course within an environment or niche but through the processes of structural coupling one changes the other and the possibilities of change that are available in the future space of the system are dependent on this relationship, its history and the co-creation that happens from there.

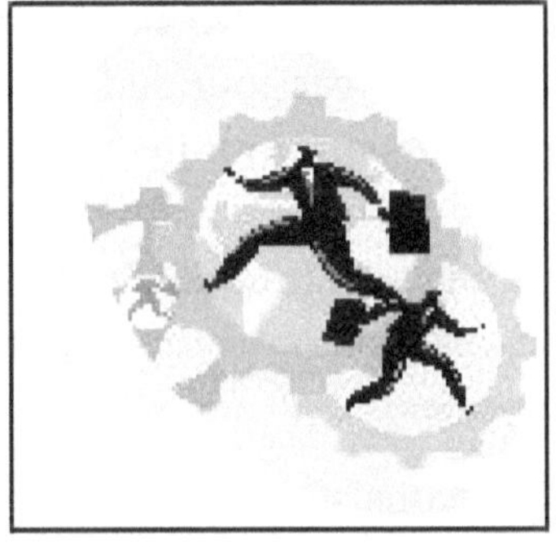

How might this look diagrammatically? The figure shows the relationship between a person and the system in an organisation. In some ways it might seem obvious that the inner world and outer worlds are interconnected but it's not often the norm. Perhaps it's difficult to see the connections if you feel either a victim of the organisation or just a small part in a much larger entity. However, as facilitators, we can notice something about our internal relationship with the system we are in and use Inner Work to unfold our view at this level.

An example

This example is taken from my work with an organisation that works in a large British city. They provide support for people who might otherwise be living in institutional environments. Their work has been highly commended and is seen as innovative, personalised, intensive and unusual. Some of the people who are supported present particular concerns because of their personal histories. They may have been or are seen as a threat to other community members or to themselves or because they have particular labels like 'personality disorder' that require varied and subtle responses not common in more institutional services. The organisation supports 46 people who live in ordinary housing in the city and employ 130 workers to do this. Because the work is often complex, in that each person may require a different set of arrangements, support levels and responses to others, they know that standardising responses is unsuccessful and often leads to failure of the service.

The service is seen as a last chance for some and therefore failure of support will in turn lead to hospitalisation of the person. The organisation was founded on a strong ethos, a commitment to inclusion for all and it believes that if the creativity is there then the answers can be found to keep everyone in community no matter what their particular needs are. The organisation aims to support everyone and not to give up on anyone.

My work with the organisation consisted of four half-day sessions with the central management team. There were two strands in this work: to explore the ways in which the team organised and supported its members, and to explore how the central team could build on that learning to discover how to better support the team leaders who were practice managers on the ground.

So far so good. The first sessions looked at some of the rank dynamics, privileges and power issues in the team but then in the middle of the work things seemed to get stuck. A process emerged that encapsulated a problematic pattern within the organisation. A series of roles emerged from within this pattern. It's important to emphasise that these are roles and to mark a difference between roles and people[10].

Remembering that as a facilitator I am now coupled with the organisation I am exploring not only my stuckness but also theirs. Two things contributed to these feelings, first was being told by the directors that the managers I was working with were not following instructions properly as had been expected (behind this was a drive for faster results – I think) and second, there was a heavy atmosphere of deadly seriousness which pervaded the work. These were evident in the conduct of the organisation's director, founder and leader. The seriousness could also be traced to a sense of the activist origins of the organisation – it was set up with an 'all means all' ethos, a desire to not fail the people they felt had been failed by society many times already. A role emerged that said something like 'don't mess up this work, the people we support must not be failed anymore'.

The primary belief here was to *do well by this belief system – to be organised, effective and highly professional* while not valued was to be *badly behaved in the sense of being a little criminal* (like the labels of some of the people they supported) – not really playing along and doing your own thing. This then led to an emergent pattern where the leader says to the managers – 'I want you to do xyz and take more responsibility and organise more things yourself', and the managers said 'of course' but then would not do what had been asked.

I also felt the seriousness of the work and felt the sense of despair in that position. Not only did I feel that this was all so deadly serious but also that I couldn't then think clearly. I felt that I was no longer free to work but also helpless, as if this was the only way of working. However, if as suggested above, the inner and outer worlds are connected within the same system then an essential method at such times has to be to use Inner Work[11].

My Inner Work

Inner Work refers to a method in Process Work in which the worker endeavours to bring awareness to various aspects of themselves, noticing the information that is contained in various channels like subtle movements or tendencies to move or in proprioceptive body signals, visual or auditory flirts and so on.

I began by remembering a conversation I had had with the organisation's director, in which she would ask me what I thought would help but would then tell me what she wanted me to do. Then, in order to help find a more second-dary part of the internal system I focused my awareness to notice what was happening in my body[12]. I remembered her seriousness and my serious response and then noticed how my body had changed with this memory. I found myself leaning forward slightly and by extending[13] this movement further I found my head making contact with the wall of my living room.

This led to a real sense of detachment, then staying with this feeling until....I felt I was going very high.... until floating above the earth I was then able to look down on myself and my work with the organisation and from this new position found a warmth and affection for what we were all engaged in but also a lightness and humour. This new mood[14] gave me a perspective on my own role and a sense of eldership[15] to myself, to the whole process and the various roles within it. This position gives a sense of detachment whilst also knowing that the position is valuable and needed and not separate from the organisa-tion. Detachment can be described as a metaskill[16]. Another way I thought of it was as a vaccine for the deadly serious-ness in the foreground.

A vaccine for deadly seriousness

Using this lightness, humour, love of all the parts and detachment as metaskills I endeavoured to work in this way in my final session with the team. It was fascinating to see the serious-ness soften as I no longer identified with that myself or felt that I had to. When asked with deadly seriousness to use such and such an approach or to do such and such an exercise in order to do the right thing with the team I was able to smile and say "no", but also to say "don't worry let's try it this way instead" whilst also feeling a warmth for the 'deadly seriousness' yet not being hypnotised by that.

A lighter atmosphere emerged for the team as a result, a lightness in dealing with each other and the emotionally charged 'edges' that often stopped managers from supporting each other and offering help to each other. The team then embarked on a long term plan to work with people they normally avoided and to ask for and receive feedback from them, asking for their help. So the vaccine for deadly serious-ness was this lightness and warmth which in turn allowed a new process to emerge where people could work together on difficult issues without feeling that to do so was a life and death matter. The original process of 'get it right this is deadly serious' was an important response to the needs of the people the organisation serves. But also, to be useful, it requires an attitude where to learn about mistakes with lightness and not to 'always to do the right thing' is OK.

Whilst writing this article I was reminded how during this period, the director would often bring her new puppy into the office. The dog became a daily visitor in the office hinting at a playful element that needed to come in and be giving more awareness in the system.

Andy Smith

is a Director with Diversity Matters Edinburgh[17] and a phase two student with RSPOPUK programme. Diversity Matters provides consultancy, training and community development services in Scotland and the U.K. Diversity Matters is a member of Altrum[18].

[1]   Audergon, J-C (2005) 'New Horizons in Body Psychotherapy - a Process Work perspective', in Totton, N (Ed.) *Handbook on New Horizons in Body Psychotherapy*, London: Open University Press

[2]   Capra, F (1996) *The web of life: A new synthesis of mind and matter* London: Harper Collins

[3]   Good Will Hunting a film by Directed by Gus Van Sant Produced by Lawrence Bender Written by Matt Damon and Ben Affleck

[4]   Kendrick, M (2001) *The Contribution Of Service Workers In Getting The Relationship 'Right' Between People With Disabilities And Their Communities*, available at www.kendrickconsulting.org

[5]   Audergon, A (2004) *The War Hotel: Psychological Dynamics in Violent Conflict*, p. 263/4 London: Whurr

[6] Midgley, M (2003) *Myths We Live By*, London: Routledge

[7] Bateson, G. (2000) *Steps to an Ecology of Mind*, pp.460-462 University of Chicago Press

[8]   Audergon, A 2004 see n. 5

[9]   Maturana, H & Valera, F (1992). *The Tree of Knowledge*, Boston: Shambhala Press

[10] Mindell, A (1997) *Sitting in the Fire : Large Group Transformation Using Conflict and Diversity*, Portland: Lao Tse Press

[11] about Inner Work see many of Arnold Mindell's books, including *River's Way: The Process Science Of The Dreambody* (1985) London and Boston: Penguin.

[12] I was greatly assisted in this Inner Work by my supervisors Julie Diamond see www.juliediamond.net and Clare Hill, Edinburgh

[13] Mindell, A 1997 see n. 10

[14] Diamond, J and Jones, L. S (2004) *A Path Made by Walking: Process Work in Practice*. Portland, Oregon: Lao Tse Press

[15] Eldership is sometimes referred to as a metaskill in Process Work and can also denote an embracing position of welcoming all sides without judgement

[16] Mindell, Amy (1994) *Metaskills: the spiritual art of therapy*. Tempe, Arizona: New Falcon 94/Lao Tse Press

[17] www.diversity-matters.co.uk

[18] Altrum is a consortium of small local organisations in Scotland committed to Inclusion and Citizenship for all. www.altrum.org.uk. is a website under construction at June 2006

Eldership and Inner Work: Working with Large Organisations

An Interview with Max Schupbach, June 2006
by Anup Karia (with Stanya Studentova)

Max Schupbach is one of the elders and co-founders of Process Work. As a teacher he embodies lightness and a deep connection to spirit and dreaming. Recently he has been meditating on, researching and teaching about the relationship between eldership[1] and leadership (see his website www.maxfacilitation.net). This coupled with his ongoing work with large organisations drew Stanya and myself to the idea to interview him on this subject in connection to Inner Work. We were thrilled when he agreed, given his immensely tight schedule.

Anup: *Max it is great to talk with you across the oceans and time zones (Max is in Portland USA and Anup is in London). Thanks for agreeing to talk about facilitation, organisational systems and dreaming.*

Max: It's a pleasure to. I love Jean-Claude and I love this idea of the book.

Anup: *Could you elucidate on the relationship between organisational work and Inner Work, and how is the Inner Work one does as a facilitator relevant to one's work with the organisation, and what's the underlying belief behind this?*

Max: Field theory in Process Work says that in a given field, your psychology and the psychology of the organisation are organised by the same forces so that the separation between your own inner process and the process of the organisation is arbitrary. The separation between where the individual ends and the organisation begins is a group process by itself. That's one of the points of the quantum mind[2]. Look at it in terms of the Big U. The Big U[3] of the organisation and you in it, your own personal myth[4] and the myth of the organisation are one and the same; they are individual musicians in the same big orchestra, playing a composition that is written by the organisational mind. Listening to it you can clearly differentiate the violin and the cello, but where exactly one ends and the other begins depends on the subjective experience of the listener, because the two instruments combine together for a whole new one. It is your awareness and the process of you and your organisation which will decide where to make the boundary at a given moment. So your Inner Work in that sense is crucial. It is like finding out the musical score by noticing what it is you are playing, or, said with a different metaphor, it is like picking up the phone and joining the conversation between you and the organisation.

Anup: *That's a great analogy, picking up on the telephone connection.*

Max: Any issues or problems that you have before you start your work in an organisation are the telephone ringing from the organisation, the myth of the organisation calling you. You have to pick up the telephone and listen to what they have to say.

Anup: *Max, as you talk about the personal myth and myth of the organisations, what draws you personally to this work?*

Max: I've been excited about organisations for a few years. I have also had a strong interest in politics, starting in childhood really. I don't know if you're aware of it but, in the beginning years of Process Work - in the early eigthies - I think I was more identified with teaching Process Work and co-creating Process Work communities in different countries in Europe and around the world. And that's been really an amazing learning experience. But then I think that maybe in the last eight years or so I got interested in communities that I had traditionally not so much connection with. I had been more connected to psychological and spiritual groups, and indigenous communities. Mainstream organisations and especially the business world had less of a pull for me. I continued to remain very interested in politics and I believed that the next step in evolution had to happen through expanding individual consciousness. And then with the arrival of worldwork[5] we as a community became much more political. But maybe the classical worldwork community was more interested in social activism, and I think I got curious initially about how to apply worldwork in big organisations, especially within the business setting.

I met some of the business people who inspired me in the way that they thought about the world as a whole. They were, and are, wonderful people and great leaders like Karin Sanvol from Norsk Hydro, Laura Conlon from IBM, and Theo Nkone from Old Mutual in South Africa, who are interested and active in changing the world at large, by supporting the role of business and improving relationships between people. They woke me up to being a worldworker with a more open mind, and applying the global worldwork categories in the business settings. Organisational development is struggling to develop more of a global theory at this point, as you probably know.

Classical organisational development or facilitation is more around a set of technologies, or an assumption about our social behaviour, it focuses on methods and technologies. But there is no consistent global theory that describes what happens within a social setting in a scientific way. General concepts like chaos theory[6], which imply an invisible order behind seemingly unstructured events, are being used in the absence of a global theory. Complex systems theory never dealt sufficiently with the observer-observed dilemma[7]. Worldwork brings a change there because it has a consistent theory, it spells out global categories, and its phenomenological approach[8] makes it easy for people to find out for themselves whether it works or not, but first and foremost it has an exact theory as to the role and experience of the observer within a system. As you know, it postulates a non-local observer role, in sync with Quantum Mechanics, and therefore implies that awareness and consequently facilitation is an ontological part of nature. So I was interested in how that applies in the business world. We have had very good experiences with business people.

Anup: *When you say there is no consistent theory that makes lots of sense to me. So one of the things that Process Work brings in is how the Inner Work of the facilitator is key.*

Max: Yes. Well it's interesting. For example, most facilitation models claim or hope to use a neutral facilitator. And the neutrality of the facilitator is stressed in many of the technologies that are around.

Anup: *Yes, I get that.*

Max: I think in worldwork we don't have so much the concept of the neutral facilitator. I think of it more as an open facilitator. 'Open' meaning open to the experience that she is having within the group but also open to the experiences that happen inside of oneself. For example, a facilitator describing organisational processes might write about this without mentioning her own experience in it. This is more of a Newtonian concept that says there is an objective organisational reality that can be written about, that is not directly linked to the personal myth of the facilitator. But then when you talk to mainstream facilitators privately they frequently talk about a lot of emotionnal and spiritual experiences they have while they are in the group and how these have been marginalised.

Now Ellen Schupbach, my partner, has done a lot of work as you know around the spiritual experience of the therapist and the facilitator[9]. Her idea is that your own inner experiences are directly linked to whatever happens in the group and form a deeper spiritual bond if you allow yourself to notice it. They can be tracked and directly used for whatever happens within the group, especially its spiritual development. All groups yearn for spiritual development and are thrilled if it happens, even if they identify with material survival. In that respect, they are like people.

Anup: *So Max, in terms of following this idea of the open facilitator, in Process Work one of the things we work with are edges (limits of our identity). I was wondering how you see a similar phenomenon happening between organisations and facilitators and if there's a way you could expand on that or if you have an example even.*

Max: Actually let me just brainstorm a little bit about it. There are many questions and topics in the background of this question. The edges of the facilitator and organisation are intimately linked. How that was or is true for me, for example, is that I used to struggle with seeing an organisation as a developing unit, where everything was meaningful as it was, and that the development had to be supported and facilitated on its own terms. I felt I had to 'change' the organisation, and frequently, the change agent who contacted me also wanted to 'change' the organisation. I had to learn that this is a great approach, but then you have to follow the process of the organisation, meaning discover how what is happening is the key to the change everyone is looking for.

As Process Work is growing up now, there are different applications and different parts of applications that are starting to be used, for example, by large organisations. Look up 'deep democracy' in Google on the internet and you will find pages and pages now of different groups and organisations, all of whom use this term. The term was originally coined by Arny Mindell in the 80s. You can see that the term has crossed over. 'Crossed over' meaning that the term is no longer used in the strict sense that it was originally developed; the original definition of deep democracy was that all voices, frameworks and states of consciousness and levels of perception that are present are equally important and need at some point or another to be represented.

However, although many groups might not use this term quite the same way, I get the impression that there's a general feeling that when people talk about deep democracy they have an intuitive sense of what was originally meant. They know it means not just a regular democracy when you vote on content, but where you feel that it goes somewhat deeper. That's why we created www.deepdemocracymovement.net as a site that would network between the various groups.

Anup: *Yes.*

Max: So I think that we're going to see more organisational work where individual aspects like the ghost role[10] will be used or picked up - most organisations that I work with, for example, particularly enjoy spotting the ghost role and find it really helpful. So some organisations, a bit like a client who comes for a session, will pick up a particular aspect of Process Work and that's as far as they'll go. So from that viewpoint, if you work as an organisational facilitator your task is to follow an organisation's process and not think that the organisation should be, 'process oriented'. That I think is a key issue in working with organisations as it is with working with people.

Anup: *That's really interesting you say that because it makes me think that I have such an attitude - seeing big corporations as needing to change in the direction that I want them to change.*

Max: Yeh – everyone does.

Anup: *What you emphasise is that, as a facilitator, you're working within their structure, not imposing something from the outside.*

Max: Yes - well everybody thinks big is bad these days. The big corporations themselves often privately tell me that they think big is bad.

Anup: *I can believe that.*

Max: You see I think there's a hole – we are not sufficiently aware that we are big corporations ourselves. And that most of us will, for example have a tendency to put our own need for more power in consensual reality[11], before our own dreaming[12]. We project our desire for power out onto the corporations. I think that's just natural. These last couple of decades has, on one level, been the age of business, and many of us see this as a major force behind politics and the shaper of our everyday perception of reality. The West interpreted – in my view partially incorrectly - the collapse of the Iron Curtain as a victory for capitalism, and only now we are starting to see trends that try to find various ways of governance and ethics for businesses and also for the way we do business globally.

Business and social activism that is focused on material rank are in fact in my view very close through that common focus. Look for example, at the basic approach of the United States towards terrorism and religious debate – it's not just in the United States but an attitude in the West. It's still largely a view point or a philosophy that says, if we help 'these people' to be materially more developed, give them more things and more access to today's twenty first century world and tools – this will change. It's like, once we alleviate economic differences those things will be worked out. The whole economic thinking is much deeper in our psychology than most of us seem to realise or would like to realise. Equating social justice with the fair distribution of material resources and seeing business as a group who hoards and monopolizes resources is the other side of the coin, where a business feels it needs to expand or beat or buy the competition in order to survive in a tough and unfair market. These values, which in many ways are very similar, are much closer to many cultures' mainstream view of what life is than many of us would like to think.

Anup: *So Max what you're saying is that even our view of social justice is based on a business way of thinking. I wonder if, as there is a 'one world' tendency in social justice movements there is a similar tendency in big businesses?*

Max: The thing is that the large fusions and mergers that create these super-organisations are, not only, but also a positive development because in the background I sense a new way of looking at competition. The corporations haven't yet figured out the fun way to do this but they're trying to by getting together and starting to think how they can collaborate instead of competing with each other. The principle of least action is constantly looking for a more fun and effortless way to live, but if you have no concepts of levels of awareness, then it is chasing your own tail. Frequently when I work with a facilitator who hasn't had much experience yet with businesses, I hear that they feel working with a business is a fundamentally different (eg in comparison with a grassroots group) experience. Certainly businesses do have different boundary conditions but otherwise it's an organisation with a myth and with people and, in that sense, it's nothing that special.

Anup: *(laughing)...makes me think how I don't identify with business and how much I project out – all these people in suits.*

Max: Yes, the dress code! We have a dress code in the Process Work community too! Our dress code (in a way) is to look as if we don't care too much about how we look. I like how Carlos Castaneda meets Don Juan[13] in a suit in a bank and he is shocked – Don Juan is wearing silk socks! Don Juan tells Castaneda – it's all about shape shifting. I love the Process oriented dress code which signals that it's important what's inside a person and that we like to be loose and informal. We find that's in the business world too, where the dress code signals that you are powerful, have a vision, and are willing to put yourself out there and make it happen.

Anup: *I want to ask you about the link between Inner Work and the self-organising principle in working with organisations.*

Max: The self-organising principle is an acceptable way of talking about 'dreaming'. Self-organisation is a term that has come out of complex systems theory. It's a euphemism because what does it mean to self-organise? It organises itself – it means, it's not organised by you – it's out of control; it doesn't necessarily dissociate. Prigogine[14] observed the principle of self-organisation as he was running up the stairs and he stumbled; as he stumbled, he saw that his feet were doing all sorts of weird things to make him balance so he didn't fall. It helped him not to fall, and he used this insight for a new understanding of the chemistry problem he was working on. That's how he came up with the concept of a self-organising principle that can bring higher degrees of order into systems, but without putting work into it as classical thermo-dynamics suggests. It means our legs coordinate themselves or are organised by something that we call dreaming. I love to remember that when I stumble all over the place. Non-equilibrium thermo-dynamics is trying to explain how this happens in detail, but this is not the point of this interview.

So when we talk about self-organising tendencies in organisations, what we're saying is the organisations themselves have a basic direction in which they are moving and that the organisations have a myth or a BIG U – which is the same. The Big U is not a higher self – but it's a direction which has its own song-line[15]. We have to discover that and then can follow it with more fun and creativity. My Inner Work as a facilitator is like listening to the music, which binds me into the dance with the organisation that hears the same music. The concept of Inner Work suggests that there is an individual inside me – working on my personal history[16] including my prejudices around whether I like or don't like business. That's true, but it is only half the truth. In addition to that it's like checking with yourself - am I hearing inside the same rhythm that others in the organisation are hearing and can we dance together with that?

Anup: *That's beautiful.*

Max: The original idea of business was relationship and communion, expressed in exchange and barter; one brought something to the other group and exchanged with what they had. First of all it was fun getting stuff which we didn't have. But it was also basic curiosity – the exchange of ideas. For example, the European colonizers in America picked up many ideas, and also many foods like corn and potatoes came from the native peoples and form now the core of staples in Europe. Because of our Euro-centric views, this never gets fully acknowledged. An African proverb says that well: 'Until the lions produce their own historian, the story of the hunt with glorify only the hunter'.

Anup: *Also the American constitution has been influenced by Iroquois (Native American tribe) ideas.*

Max: Yes, exactly, the five Iroquois Nations, called the League of Peace and Power, were based on a concept of spiritual union of different communities and had a central influence on the American Constitution. Many European democratic ideas were expanded and rejuvenated by Native American democratic ideas.

Anup: *Now Max, one more question to ask you; in your view what is the difference between an elder and a leader?*

Max: Yes, this is what I'm passionate about at the moment, for me the next step in the leadership theory is, what eldership is and what it means. To use an example, the USA, like it or not, have an enormous amount of consensus reality rank, meaning access to material resources and military power. The sheer potential would give them a regulatory effect on the world, even if they never use it. Some people consider this a problem. But in my view, this alone is not an issue. The problem arises when it comes to awareness of this power and communicating to the rest of the world why and how it is being used and with what goal. Also, socio-economic rank is not the only rank a nation has.

The USA, to stay with this example, have for example also multiversity rank by being a society that is largely made up of immigrants from the whole world. I envision for example a mega event between Arabic American, Israeli American, Jewish American and Muslim American groups, and everyone else who is called to be part of it, working on their relationships and televising it. Notice that all these groups have a common bond, the word 'American' and also many of the differences of the Middle Eastern group. I think something like that would help.

Anup: *This demonstrates that we need to embody the leader we want the Government to be.*

Max: In my vision I also see business doing something similar. You know the Bill and Melinda Gates foundation have just given twenty two billion dollars for health care in Africa. That's great! But I would like to see an even bigger vision from them. I would, especially, expect Bill Gates to understand that the world needs a different operating system. He has after all created the most popular computer operating system in the world. Twenty two billion dollars is a great start, it can alleviate a lot of suffering, but we also need a different way of thinking about eldership and relationships. If you have windows, you want it to open every file that is on your hard disk. If some files wouldn't open, or were all having problems, you would not spend all your money on changing those files, but also work on the operating system that can't access them. Some of the money should go into studying mindsets and attitudes of the 'helpers' and how to process them; they are the equivalent of operating systems, so to speak.

Anup: *This example really illustrates the difference between elder and leader. Talking with you feels like such a feast!*

Max: I like your questions because they help me in trying to organise my own thinking about it.

Anup: *Thank you. I would like to go back to the question about edges. We were talking about edges of the facilitator and the organisation. I wonder if you could explain how this dynamic happens in terms of shared edges.*

Max: A shared edge with a client that means that you are on the edge and the client may be on the same edge, so your work can't go further, till one or the other of you notices that. Would you agree?

Anup: *Yes.*

Max: Yes, that is why working in teams is often useful, it helps us notice our edges and once we notice them, the edge of the organisation becomes visible also. But I think that the biggest edge that I see, is to think that you can go and actually help large groups, and to believe that a shift of the mindset can truly give you the leverage to change reality. I know for myself, that I think changing the mindset is the easiest but making it happen, the practical application, is the biggest problem, but I also know from experience, that it is in fact most often the other way round.

Anup: *Yeah, what would you say is the best way to change this mindset; what do I as a facilitator need to do?*

Max: The best way to develop yourself, in my view, is to like what you do and be interested in your client, her community and background and her ideas and experiences. That is true for working with organisations also, and also the business community. I think that is the biggest issue, that the more you start to work with mainstream organisations and in the background feel 'business is not good, government is no good', they will feel it, and that's the edge that you need to work on; but none of that is any different from what everybody already knows when they work with an individual client.

Anup: *Yes, that's the same principle; that really helps Max, thank you so much.*

Thanks to Andy Smith for helping in formulating some of the questions; and to Gina Clayton for her help with transcribing.

Max Schupbach, Ph.D.

is a co-founder of Process Work Centres in many countries. Max coaches leaders and executive teams from diverse organisations and countries, and develops and implements organisationwide change management processes. He conducts open forums, and has facilitated leadership trainings in the Australian Aboriginal and indigenous American Communities. He is the founder and director of the Lava Rock Clinic.

www.maxfacilitation.net

[1] Eldership - doesn't relate so much to age, but to the complex ability of a leader to communicate across hierarchies, and to influence across communities. An elder understands and values human development on this earth, and sees her or himself, nature, and others, bound together in learning and growing. See: Schupbach M. Glossary http://www.maxfacilitation.net/glossary_topic.asp?glo_id=23 (accessed July 22, 2006). See also: Audergon A. 2005. *The War Hotel. Psychological Dynamics of Violent Conflict.* London: Whurr/Whiley. P. 255

[2] See: Mindell A. 2000. *Quantum Mind. The Edge between Physics and Psychology.* Portland. Oregon: LaoTse Press. p. 585

[3] See: Mindell A. 2000. *Dreaming While Awake. Techniques for 24-hour Lucid Dreaming.* Charlottesville: Hampton Roads Publishing. P. 199-209

[4] See: Diamond J and Jones L S. 2004. *A Path made by Walking: Process Work in Practice.* Portland. Oregon: LaoTse Pres. p. 148-149

[5] Worldwork is a new paradigm for working with change within the complete spectrum of organisational and communal life. At the centre of worldwork's philosophical framework are awareness and the study of consciousness. See: Schupbach M. *Worldwork – Transformation in Organisations, Communities, Business, and the Public Space.* http://www.maxfacilitation.net/ov.pdf (accessed July 23. 2006)

[6] Gleick J. 1998. *Chaos: The Amazing Science of the Unpredictable.* London: Vintage.

[7] See: Mindell A. 2000. *Quantum Mind.* p. 234-235 (n 2 above)

[8] Phenomenological approach means describing what is happening rather then explaining and interpreting it. See also: Lester S. 1999. *An*

Introduction to Phenomenological Research.
http://www.devmts.demon.co.uk/resmethy.htm (accessed July 22, 2006)

[9]   Schupbach E. 2004. *The Gold at the End of the Rainbow: A Hermeneutic Study of Therapist Spiritual Experience.* Dissertation. PW Center in Portland, Oregon.

[10]   A ghost role is a role in the group that is not directly spoken for but whose effects are nonetheless felt in the group atmosphere and can be seen in the behaviour of group members who react to the ghost role. See: http://www.maxfacilitation.net/glossary topic.asp?glo id=21(accessed July 22, 2006). See also: Mindell A. 2002. *The Deep Democracy of Open Forums. Practical Steps to Conflict Prevention and Resolution for Family, Workplace, and World.* Charlottesville: Hampton Roads Publishing. p.37

[11]   Consensus Reality is the reality that is agreed upon by the majority as being valid and true within a specific culture or group. See:

http://www.maxfacilitation.net/glossary topic.asp?glo id=6 (accessed July 22, 2006). See also: Mindell A. 2000. *Dreaming While Awake. Techniques for 24-hour Lucid Dreaming* p.46-52 (n 3 above)

[12]   Dreaming is a term used to define any experience that is outside of a person's conscious control. Process Work views dreaming in a way that is similar to the Australian Aboriginal concept. See: http://www.maxfacilitation.net/glossary topic.asp?glo id=7 (accessed July 22, 2006). See also: Mindell A. 2002. *The Deep Democracy of Open Forums.* p.117 (n.10 above)

[13]   Castaneda C. 1974. *Tales of Power.* New York: Simon and Schuster. p 103.

[14]   Prigogine I. and Stengers I. 1984. *Order out of Chaos.* New York: Bantam Books.

[15]   Songlines emerge as invisible pathways connecting all over Australia, made of songs which tell of the creation of the land. A key concept of aboriginal culture is that they and the land are one. See also: Songlines. Wikipedia. http://en.wikipedia.org/wiki/The Songlines (accessed July 23. 2006)

[16]   See: Mindell A. 2004 *The Quantum Mind and Healing.* Charlottesville: Hampton Roads Publishing. p 188-190

The Missing Elder

By Mark O'Connell

In 1982, when I was 18 years old, I drove three of my closest friends to the Nenthead Green Moon Festival in Cumbria. I had taken the previous year after finishing school for music and other kinds of 'experimentation', all of which involve altered states to one degree or another. I didn't know that in one weekend at Nenthead my entire way of seeing the world would be turned on its head. I was on the threshold of a major life transition, which would reverberate through my twenties, thirties and now into my forties. This weekend would shockingly awaken me to the spiritual in life while affording me no eldership at all. It would only be many years later in discovering Process Oriented Psychology that I would begin to meet the eldership I had so needed at that time.

I drove my father's expensive car into the centre of that festival, an unconscious symbol of my privileged middle class upbringing, and a naïve sense of security. It was soon after erecting our tents that we were found by some festival-goers, in whose company I will always remember the trickster. He offered us some cookies supposedly laced with hash, and as we ate he began to play with our perceptions, pretending to have accidentally swallowed a pin.

It was soon after this that a veil parted. The beginning of an experience which would later be framed by my relatives as 'only the effect of the LSD', but nevertheless as real to me then as it is to me now in my recollections. I became profoundly aware of all manner of influences and tendencies. I realised that my friends and I were being pulled-upon as if by invisible strings. Now as a Process Worker I consider this to have been my first conscious experience of a 'field' organising my experience. My friends were enjoying their altered states and were readily drawn out into the festival, pulled upon by the music, lights and people around them, while I became terrified of how unconsciously manipulated we were all becoming by this invisible field. I started to feel out of control and wanted my friends around me. I then recall picking-up a guitar and playing two notes over and over again creating a trance-like magnetism upon my friend Peter. In this way I held him close to me inside our tent.

Later that evening we ventured out, and I soon became aware that through all the different folk music, Hawkwind rock music, sounds of people and generators, I was experiencing 'one sound' playing behind and unifying all of the other sounds. A kind of auditory 'Unus Mundus' experience in which everything was One, however I remained terrified. This unifying of sound and of vision was to revisit me in flashbacks for many years to come, while walking in the night, or riding a motorcycle through the busy streets of Brighton. And eventually I began to enjoy these moments and they became awesome times of wonder in which awareness, dreaming and every-day sense of reality seemed to flow together. Such experiences have become increasingly familiar through Process Work when the nature of a given moment leads the way.

My girlfriend was really enjoying herself listening to a rather fabulous (in retrospect) folk band playing in a circle around a large campfire. I asked her to come back to the tent with me, as I was becoming frightened again. She agreed to come, and then she told me that she was experiencing being in two places at the same time, both with me in the tent, and still sitting around the campfire. Awesome to me now, terrifying to me then. I became acutely anxious and at this point, sitting with her in the tent I began to hear a cloven-hoofed Devil dancing around us, playing wildly on his violin, and I sensed his intent to kill me. This same dreamfigure, or maybe from a shamanic point of view my Double, has appeared to me periodically at each of my Process Work exams, and over time I realising that he is truly my own wild and creative spirit seeking out my awareness through my bodily symptoms, behind my fear of death, through my sexuality, and in the depths of my love of music. Recently, working at a residential school and children's home, I overcame a deep sense of unease with the place by playing guitar and welcoming my musical-self into the workplace.

Driving away from the festival at the end of the weekend I could feel the pull of the area on my body even many miles away at my home in Newcastle-upon-Tyne. My family tried to support me by explaining the experience away as unreal, but for me a new sense of reality was dawning, and it was painful for my perceptions to be questioned. Shortly afterwards I moved to University in Sussex with an accompanying fear of the smell of incense, often feeling like I would fall into the night sky when I looked up or that I would fall out through open windows. I was also experiencing powerful highs and lows in my moods. It was Transcendental Meditation which at this point helped me to ground myself and was the beginning of a long spiritual search.

In 1991 I had a powerful and bodily-felt fantasy that I was about to die and it was exactly after this time that I discovered Process Oriented Psychology and began to study for the diploma. Jean-Claude has been a central elder figure for me in my development as a Process Worker. This was the kind of eldership I had so much needed and yet was entirely missing during my teenage experience at Nenthead. My first experience of working with Jean-Claude was in the middle of a group in Devon in which one part of me was desperately trying to wake-up another part of me which kept disappearing into a trance. The awakening of awareness has been a central feature of our work ever since. My present day supervision with Jean-Claude seems to be more focused upon awakening the elder within me. It is only now, 24 years after Nenthead that I begin to understand that weekend's experience as a field or life-myth seeking unfolding and awareness: wild, creative and primitive forces of nature seeking relationship with 'civilised' man: a privileged young man unconsciously seeking relationship with his deeper nature. The 'trickster', the 'devil', the terrified teenager, the relatives who doubted my altered states and dreamlike experiences, and the missing elder, are all parts of a/my Dreambody seeking awareness.

Through Jean-Claude I repeatedly learn about field theory. That when you move into a given situation, everything you feel can be understood as a role in relation to other roles and 'ghost-like' roles which are also present in that situation. It is easy to become identified or taken by one particular role forgetting that it is part of a broader field and so it becomes important to notice how your momentary experience is a partial expression of the whole field. Jean-Claude reminds the 'missing elder' in me to facilitate the field, through supporting its different aspects while at the same time supporting my own perceptions.

Here I try to introduce some of the missing eldership and facilitation to the roles in the field of my 1982 experience:

Devil: (Dancing and playing violin) Hold me just a little bit, love me just a little bit [dances closer]

Teenager: I'm scared. I was confident I knew how the world worked, but now you have thrown me. I'm like a boat tossed on a wild sea. I don't know if I can deal with these new realities.

Elder: This wild Devil wants more contact with you, and you are terrified. Maybe it's not the right time? What should we do?

Teenager: No I am interested. But shaken.

Adult: I am angry about a society which has no elders. How can young people in the West discover their deeper nature, without going mad?

Devil: I'm just going wild for a good time. Dance with me! Play with me!

Teenager (to Trickster): I thought everyone could be pretty well trusted until I met you.

Trickster: Glad to be part of waking you up.

Devil: Hey trickster I'm going to kick you across this 'field' unless you find better ways! You are just playing with him and don't care about his growth.

Teenager: Wow thanks!

Elder: Teenager seems to be enjoying a bit of Devilish support, and just learnt not to be so open and trusting. The Devil is not so isolated any more. What else needs to happen?

Doubting Relatives: None of this is real except for Teenager having a bad trip. There's a good explanation for it. It's just irrational and there is no proof for it.

Teenager and the Devil: You've dismissed us for far too long. You have the broad support of society. Thinking you have the rights on reality, and disregarding dreams and altered states. It may be scary for you to consider other perceptions than your own, but we suffer and are isolated when you continually dismiss us like that.

Elder: Well many in this 'field' have spoken, and there may be roles and spirits who have not yet spoken. Shall we use this deadline of midnight on the 18th June 2006 for articles for Jean-Claude's book 'Far In, Far Out,' to be written, to draw this process to a close? Thank you to all those who have spoken, and to those who remained silent. And a big thank you to Jean-Claude on his 60th birthday, for his teachings, eldership and support of all of our unfolding.

Mark O'Connell
 is a practising Process Worker and founding member of RSPOPUK. His current interests are: working with adolescents, school community development, field theory, the creative process, and sustainability. He and his wife Marina run a small training centre for sustainability in East Anglia called 'The Apricot Centre',
www.apricotcentre.co.uk

Edge – Mindell's term for the momentary and long-term limits of our identity, where growth can take place.

Field – Here meaning the organising pattern behind any event or situation. One way in which the field becomes known to us is through roles and ghost roles.

Dreambody – Originally the connection between dreams and body feelings, Mindell's Dreambody concept has now expanded to include the organising dreamfield which patterns experience at many levels.

Role – Roles are identifications occurring at an everyday level and through our dreaming process.

Ghost Role – A role which is not yet manifest but which nevertheless affects us and is implicit in the atmosphere, language, gossip, and signals of a given situation.

Dreamfigure – A role occurring at a dreaming level.

Eldership – Mindell describes this as being in touch with the direction of our deepest nature

Unus Mundus – A Jungian term referring to the experience of things as simultaneously separate and unified, in which the duality of inner and outer events no longer exists. Becoming at one with the collective unconscious.

Reality – Referring to what is believed or experienced to be actual or true.

162

Dialoguing
Across Irreconcilable Differences

By Jayne Stewart

I was sexually abused by my father from when I was 3 until I was 12. I survived the abuse by disassociating - my body stayed present but my conscious mind split off and 'forgot'. When my son was 3 I began to recover my memories and confronted my father, he denied the abuse and continues to do so. I survived the remembering, by splitting in a different way - I cut off from my father.

For a long time I focused on my rage, I wanted revenge, to punish, even to kill. I made my father wholly bad, 'other'. At least I tried to. But I was abused by someone who also loved me, and I loved him. I have not been able to cut myself off totally, because to do so would have been to cut myself off from too much of myself. Gradually the pain of the love between us also took shape. I grieved that this abuse was done to me not by a stranger, but by someone who knew and loved me.

In September 1998 I visited my father for the first time in 6 years. My journey back to my father's door has been one of reclamation and integration, reclaiming all of my experience in order to become whole. During that first visit we began to dialogue across our irreconcilable differences, and have continued to do so over the past 8 years.

In January 2002 I attended a Process Oriented Psychology workshop on Conflict Resolution facilitated by Jean-Claude and Arlene Audergon called Mountain Peak Mountain Path. We were given an 'Injustice and Accountability' checklist and an exercise, based on the work of Arnold Mindell, to do as a way of bringing more awareness to these issues. Several months after the workshop I decided to use the checklist to look at my conflict with my father.

Injustice and Accountability Checklist

(From an exercise by Arlene & Jean-Claude Audergon, used with permission. A similar chart can be found in Arlene's book, The War Hotel[1])

When we feel we have been unjustly treated we may want some of the following, often initially we want the things near the top of the list, but if we do not receive them we start to want the things near the bottom.

1. Acknowledgement that the event happened
2. Acknowledgement of your version of events
3. Recognition of the other person's part in contributing to it and a sign that they understand how what they did affected you
4. An authentic 'felt' apology
5. Recognition of their misuse of their rank or power
6. Them to move beyond their feeling of guilt towards a recognition of responsibility and accountability
7. A commitment to change
8. An actual change in behaviour
9. Reparations
10. Punishment
11. That the hurt and humiliation that we felt be inflicted on them.
12. Removal of the person from society
13. The person to be killed

I went through the checklists from mine and my father's opposite points of view:

1. My father denies his abusive behaviour.
2. He totally denies my version of events
3. He does not admit his part in causing my distress, this denial makes me feel worse
4. Far from apologising my father says *he* has forgiven *me* for all the distress my accusations have caused him!
5. He has no awareness of power issues re adult:child interactions or the power of denying another person's experience or the rank pulling involved in claiming GOD on his side
6. I once asked him for some money to help finance my studies and as an acknowledgement of how much his behaviour has cost me in terms of therapy and lost income and he said he couldn't give me any because 'other people' would interpret it as an admission of guilt!
7. No need to change because he didn't do it
8. Interesting that 7 is, in fact, not true he *has* changed his behaviour. He has made no attempt to have any contact with any of his grandchildren except under the conditions we lay down and he never spends any time alone with children. However this was only after my brother, who my father also abused, discovered that he was looking after his step-daughter's young son, and we reported him to Child Protection Services.
9. I often used to fantasise about getting some money from him (see 6).
10. – 13. After we reported my father to social services the police initiated an investigation, took statements from us and questioned my father. My brother wanted a guilty verdict to gain acknowledgement

from an outside authority that the abuse happened and to punish my father and remove him from society by having him sent to prison. The Director of Public Prosecutions however decided there was insufficient evidence for a successful prosecution, as siblings did not count as independent witnesses! I had mixed feelings about the court case: they can be traumatic events and I was not sure that sending my father to prison would help any of us. I have, however, hated him and often imagined hurting or killing him. My brother sent angry letters to my father's second wife and to the church, the school and others in the village where he lives, and finally my brother killed *himself* in September 1999.

From my father's world all this looks very different:
Out of the blue comes a false accusation of childhood sexual abuse, first from his daughter and then from his son. They cut off from him completely and deny him access to his grandchildren. His ex-wife and his other two children side against him. His younger daughter rarely brings her children to see him, never stays overnight or leaves her children with him unsupervised and he is no longer invited to stay at her house.

He is reported to social services and his step-daughter is informed that her son should not be left alone with him. He is arrested and questioned by the police. His son sends vindictive letters to him, his second wife and members of the local community. He is afraid that he may lose his job, his second family and his place as a respected member of church and community. His son commits suicide and he is blamed and not allowed to go to the funeral. This is the stuff of nightmares!

The checklist:

1. His son and daughter deny their abusive behaviour, they agree that these events happened but claim that it is his own responsibility.
2. They totally deny his version of events and say *he* is in denial
3. They do not admit their part in causing his distress and say it is self inflicted which makes him feel worse
4. Far from apologising his daughter says she cannot forgive him since he won't admit there is anything to forgive!
5. She has no awareness of the power her accusations have to ruin his life.

At that point I stopped abruptly and didn't look at the piece again for a long time.

In July 2002 following the death of a friend I drove out into countryside intending to feel the earth and some ancient rock under my feet and instead 'found myself' outside my father's house for the first time in 3 years. I surrendered to the mysterious part of me/God/Spirit and knocked on his door.

As usual when I arrive unannounced he began chatting about family members I hadn't seen for years so I reminded him that I hadn't seen him for years and I didn't know when I would again and asked what we might really want to talk about. Then we spoke about spirituality, dreams and irreconcilable differences but nothing we had not touched on before.

As time to leave approached I kept wondering what Spirit had in mind? Then I started talking about the Mountain Path Mountain Peak workshop and suddenly I knew why I was there. I said: "Without in any way changing my own version of our shared history I want to apologise to you for all the distress my actions have caused you…", my dad interrupted me waving his arms and protesting that it was not him but those around him who had been hurt.

A very strong silence followed whilst I waited, struggling to sense what next, after what felt like a rejection of a really deep gift! Then my step mother thanked me and we hugged tearfully. I explained that it felt more important to me that the suffering on both sides ended than that we carry on fighting about what the 'truth' was/is. My dad was crying too and offered me his hand across the table; we haven't touched each other for a very long time. I went round and hugged him and then he whispered, very quietly, "Forgive me if I have caused you any suffering", which is the only acknowledgement I have ever had that he has hurt me in any way.

In Jan 2006 I sent a version of what I have written above to the Forgiveness Project (http://www.theforgivenessproject.com) which aims to reframe the debate about how individuals and communities can learn to celebrate difference, over-come divi-sion and foster positive social change. They asked me to write a piece specifically for their website. Then in May they asked me if I would be willing to take part in a series of '3 Minute Wonder' programmes on the theme of Forgiveness. I told my father that I was going to do the programme and that I wanted to take care of him in the way that I did it. After walking and talking together for several hours he gave the project his blessing. The resulting film will was shown on Channel 4 in the first week of July to coincide with the anniversary of the July 7th London Tube bombings.

Reflecting now I realise that there was something right about stopping at point 5 of my father's side of the check-list. At the time I was disturbed by how potentially power-ful what I was learning was and afraid of the implications.

By apologising to him for the hurt that I have caused him and by taking his feelings into account in the making of the TV programme I have used my power and my psychological and spiritual rank in a responsible and accountable way.

I am also modelling aspects of responsibility that were missing when the abuse happened I take responsibility for my actions as an adult and acknowledge that the choices I made caused suffering on the other side. I actively seek out and listen to the other person's experiences. I apologise and modify my behaviour. And I give thought to how I can follow my own desires and still protect and relate to the other person.

All of these issues relate not only to the abuse that happened in the privacy of my bedroom but also to the abuses that we, as a society, perpetrate in the world. We invade each other at all levels. We all need to take responsibility for breaking cycles of revenge and beginning dialogues across irreconcilable differences. And for telling all of our truth: the vulnerability and the strength, the love and the hate, the pain and the Joy. And for noticing they co-exist within each of us rather than making some of us totally innocent and others of us totally guilty.

As individuals we may be innocent but collectively we are responsible for creating the conditions in which sexual abuse flourishes. In terms of the checklist as a society we acknowledge that sexual abuse happens but we still prefer to think of it as something that is done by strangers, not by people like us, ordinary people who love each other. Nor do we recognise that our collective behaviour contributes to it. For example the restrictive social norms we create around sexuality and intimacy.

Dialoguing across irreconcilable differences creates the possibility for more intimate, mysterious and exciting meetings. Intimacy comes from meeting the 'other' both inside and out-side of ourselves and greeting them with respect and curiosity rather than suspicion and blame. Such meetings transcend our current socially defined limits and yet have clearer and more secure boundaries.

There are people who say, to me *and* to my father, "If what you say is really true then you would not want to have anything to do with him/her". Choose between being whole and being believed. And in that moment the complexity, the vulnerability and the strength of our current relationship become invisible, inadmissible.

Maintaining the strong polarisation between victim and perpetrator keeps us from moving beyond our feelings of guilt towards recognition of our collective responsibility and accountability (checklist 6). If I am to be believed I am only allowed to be a victim. No wonder it is so hard for me to let go of my attachment to my victim status. It is society's attachment too and it keeps me stuck. The rigid polarity only recognises my pain and vulnerability and puts all the strength, power and control with the abuser and that makes it difficult for me to express my strength or make choices or relate positively to my own power. And it makes it difficult for my father to admit to his vulnerability and pain and to take responsibility for his actions. We all need the common ground of our humanity.

In continuing to relate to my father and the dreaming level of the mysterious process between us, which in consensus reality is called 'abuse', I am honouring the humanity of some-one who, as a society, we consider bad, evil or just plain wrong, and by treating him with respect and protecting him from violence, I am picking up my rank and using it to take responsibility both as an individual and as a member of society.

In writing this my hope is that my experience will not only be of value to me and to my father but will also be inspiring for others and help us, both individually and collectively, move beyond cycles of revenge towards more deeply democratic ways of relating.

With Love and Gratitude to everyone who has made this possible.

Jayne Stewart

has studied Process Work for seven years. It enriches her life and work in many different ways both practically and spiritually. She is passionate about Worldwork and Deep Democracy and is always looking for creative ways to use her personal experience to demonstrate that the personal is deeply political.

Jayne Stewart is a pen name.

[1]   Audergon, A (2005) *The War Hotel: Psychological Dynamics in Violent Conflict.* London: Whurr/ John-Wiley, 2005. p.45
see also: Mindell A (2000) *The Leader as Martial Artist.* Portland OR: Lao Tse Press, and
Mindell A (1995) *Sitting in the Fire.* Portland OR: Lao Tse Press

Once Upon a Second

By David Clark

Second by second
minute by minute
hour upon hour
day after day
week after week
month after month
season following season following season
year in year out
through century after century
aeons upon aeons

Yet this
very moment
here
now
unrepeatable
unrepeatable
unrepeatable

David Clark

has been a potter, interior decorator/designer and poet, self-publishing a book of collaged poems entitled Stellations. He initially trained in Transpersonal psychology in London where he has a private practice. For the last 16 years has been studying the development of Process Work, of which, for 7 years, he was the UK co-ordinator.

seaside, Stanya Studentova

Accidentally on Purpose
An Extract from the manuscript 'Nothing Came from Walking'

By Conor McKenna

This is my third week on the island of Gozo and today I'm after somewhere new to walk to. I had read about the world famous Ta' Pinu Basilica, so decided to go and have a look at it. To get to it, I walked towards the small town of Gharb. Three quarters of the way there I took a left turn towards The Basilica, got there, looked at it and walked on – special for some but not for me. Further round, made my way to Gharb town and from there I again joined up with the road back to Victoria, doing a sort of keyhole journey – up, around and back. At one point I sat for a rest, sat on a low wall in the shade to cool off. It was then that it must have happened. I parted company with the digital camera, my new toy, my pride and joy. It was like losing part of myself, I couldn't believe the anguish. The reaction to losing it was way over the top. I discovered the loss when I returned to my apartment, looked in all the pockets of the rucksack, under the table, in the bag again, under cushions, under the table, etc, etc, etc. Gone, I couldn't believe it. Soon I was sitting in a taxi and returning to the spot. No camera there–how could there be? An obvious camera on a wall would hardly enjoy a long rest, even on a religious island. From the 'bad place', the squat wall, the hole in the world, I walked the route back to Victoria - about four miles - with no sign of it, no sign of my precious third eye. I checked the police station later and also for several days after, with no result. Where the externalisation experiences now? Where the empty monk? Where the great feeling of eternity, the creative song lines that bubbled out of me, the internal silence? All that work and transformation that manifested on this island is now gone, none of it important now – I've lost my camera and that's everything!!! First the keys, now the camera, how could I be so stupid, what sort of head have I got? I just threw away £300, how could I be so unfortunate, so absentminded, so brainless?

While walking back home to Marsalforn I rack my brain trying to remember what I did to lose it, obsessively going over and over the sequence of events. There are attempts to reason things through, incessant thinking about the consequences of the loss, criticising myself on the one hand and trying to defend myself on the other, all the time I'm living in hope that it will somehow turn up. I try to tell myself that nothing's ever been found in such a state, but it doesn't work. I continue criticising myself, taking other un-related crimes into account to support the verdict and pronounce the sentence.

As I walk the dusty road, cars speed by forcing me off and making me furious. I continue making judgements, passing sentence and imprisoning myself and then do it all over again; guilt is pronounced for being so egotistical, having attachments to objects, being acquisitive and more – much more. Another car passes with locals laughing and shouting something out of the window.

'Piss off,' I mumble, 'for all I know you yobbos took it, wouldn't be surprised if they started taking pictures of me.' I spit out expletives and then switch back and beat myself up again. 'You gobble up everything, you're so petty min-ded, everything that you touch or comes through you, you use to further yourself - gobble, gobble, gobble, you're like a praying mantis.' How I got to that attitude through losing the camera I don't know, but it felt like my ego was a praying mantis – ego gobbling everything in sight, as if the world was there for me alone.

Then a different kind of thought came: 'Strange idea, my mind as a praying mantis where did that come from?' I'd wandered into a different awareness outside my torrid mind, a different voice that used words like gobble and praying mantis, not words belonging to my normal vocabulary. In the moment of recalling 'gobble, gobble, gobble', I immediately felt, saw and held in my awareness a praying mantis. I some-how stumbled across and captured a hunter camouflaged in my thoughts. Another thought occurred.

'If the praying mantis is the ego, then what's the prey? If there is a predator around then there should be some-thing preyed on. They usually go together.'

In an instant the realisation hit me, I woke up – Christ, it eats ME! It eats me when I criticise myself, eats me when I call myself egotistical, call myself stupid. The realisation dawns that I've been setting myself up on a platter all my life. When I judge myself then I'm the prey, when I doubt myself or pull myself to pieces, I'm being eaten at that moment. When I concern myself about what others think of me, I put myself in the trap - give them my awareness, my autonomy and in that way, I'm also eaten. Slurp, slurp, a long invisible tongue appears out of nowhere picking off my words and nobody is any the wiser except that I feel dissatisfied, incomplete and wretched. The praying mantis, on the other hand, is totally egotistical and self-centred and is completely at peace with that, wouldn't even think about it – eat, gobble, eat, gobble, yum, yum. It's obvious that the praying mantis has the better part of the deal. In criticising myself I have the choice - being me or a praying mantis, I either identify with being criticised or enjoy criticising while staying hidden and protected.

There are just two positions: I'm either the prey or the praying mantis. I know which one I'm going for - the self-centred egotist who needs no one except himself. To become the praying mantis I will need to sharpen up as a hunter, a stalker, a predator. This is inner egotism and requires obscurity to survive, becoming obscure even unto myself, without history, hidden in ordinary reality, ready to pounce on life. This spirit is a secret lover, a devourer of awareness. It's a praying bishop, a divine parasite, it's God's chameleon and the devil's camouflage. It is, too, man's liberation and man's destruction, the unseen enemy that is so close that we call it 'I'. Shakespeare, it seems to me, represented this process in the figure of Iago, the secret creator of all the destruction and death throughout the play 'Othello'. It is either the destroyer or the teacher that will kill or transform you into the supreme hunter of eternity, continually sensing, stalking, and capturing everlasting freedom through blending with the environment.

With this insight I suddenly have all the awareness of a praying mantis mind. The praying mantis does nothing but sit in our thoughts, being them. It is awareness that tunes in and becomes every thought we have. It is 'non-doing'. The praying mantis never gets eaten because it is never differentiated, always camouflaged, always safe. I caught it eating my thoughts when I was angry with myself. I was reactionary, differentiated, working against myself, and the praying mantis was ingesting the whole thing, gobble, gobble, gobble. In be-coming the praying mantis, it all became simply awareness, neutral, part of me – 'Blonde on Blonde', as the singer said.

To catch a praying mantis we simply need to be aware of our thoughts, no more, no wondering about them, no analysing, no searching. In that way we are doing more of what we're already doing, but consciously. It's a simple thing - accepting oneself consciously the way we are is a good bet, makes me the concealed predator while my quarry stands out in relief seeking even greater different-tiation. All this is the way of the praying mantis.

I felt so safe and with such inner confidence that I wanted to kiss something. So I took myself off to the hills and eventually, after an hour or so, sat down next to a beautiful little thistle - yellow, feminine, receptive - pillowed by the rough ground. In this place thistles don't have stems, the blossoms sit on the soil receptive of any insects, even a foot couldn't damage it. The flower enthralled me with its beauty, pulled in all my awareness. This unassuming flower sat there as though pinned to the earth, pinned like a buttonhole for some unknown marriage. The message it gave was love; it was just there giving it to the world – nothing hidden or obscure about it, nothing camouflaged except that we don't usually notice weeds. The thistle shone with the security and safety of being inconsequential. In a way it was just as hidden as the praying mantis.

I sat next to the flower, both of us quiet. I think it was glad to be next to me, glad to be observed and I felt a gentle inner relaxation. In the stillness something caught my attention off to the side. I sensed something had moved, but when I looked, there was nothing there. Then another movement and I saw what it was. About three feet away was a long, slender, light green stick - one that moved. There it was and I couldn't believe it - who would? Right in front of me was a real, breathing praying mantis. It hung there on the stem of a dead, brown weed, struggling very slowly upwards, more stopped than moving, no movement at all if I moved. It was surreptitiously reaching for the lower branches of a short, green bush just above. As I observed, it became still – a green branch on a dead stem, incongruent, exposed, caught.

This was the first time that I had seen a praying mantis and although delighted and surprised, given my experience earlier, it seemed a natural discovery, could have expected it even. This discovery was no coincidence; I'm on the edge between a dreaming world and consensus reality, the edge of two paradigms. The dreaming world is revealing something 'accidentally on purpose'. I felt that some organising principle - a praying mantis spirit - was involved in this discovery, and in the loss of the camera, too. It created the criticism, produced the words 'gobble, gobble, gobble,' and now here it is, the physical praying mantis. As the Australian Aboriginals say, I seem to be in 'Praying Mantis Dreaming'.

Watching this fascinating creature, I became interested in why it moved so slowly and wondered how fast it could move. It was almost hanging upside down on the thin stem; a stem that could hardly survive a puff of wind never mind a three inch bishop-like devourer of insects. I inched imperceptibly closer, stalking a master-stalker, and after some minutes eventually touched its tail. As I made contact, it moved with such speed that it was instantaneously here, then there, so fast that my eyes couldn't catch the sequence. Then it returned to its frozen state again, commencing its gentle struggle upwards only after it felt safe. There we were, both playing the game of stillness and movement.

As I watched, it eventually reached the green bush and became perfectly camouflaged, settling down and miraculously transforming into a branch and leaf, to all intents and purposes – gone, if only I had my camera! I had happened upon it because it was in an exposed position on the brown soil. This was the second time that I had happened across this predator today! The movement against the background revealed it, so it had no choice but to advance as slowly as possible towards safety. As a delicate animal, speed and blending are both its weapons and its defences.

This praying mantis process in the ordinary everyday world hunts insects, but in the world of consciousness it preys on thought, preys on self-criticism, gobbles up the self-attacks. Such a voracious appetite keeps one in a state of low self-esteem, keeps one the victim, the prey. But to capture an internal praying mantis is to become it, and to become it is the transformation from being a victim. However, you don't capture it externally and internally in the same day by accident, it's a coincidence that had more than meaning, it had purpose too – I was somehow given this experience. The praying mantis revealed itself as a partner in awareness-seeking. To put it the other way around, however, I'm thinking that I'm discovering a praying mantis but actually I feel it is transforming itself into me - extending itself into the physical world.

The term 'survival of the fittest' was always a rather negative way of seeing natural processes. Is it not better to say 'the triumph of awareness'? In nature we witness the savagery of animals in the fight for survival but on the level of awareness, behind such encounters, nothing is lost and everything is gained. 'Praying mantis knowledge' says that to become a praying mantis you would do well to drop your old knowledge of yourself. It is dangerous to self-examine because you don't know who is hunting that knowledge. It says: remain obscure, even to yourself, drop your history and identity, leave those who know you because that knowing reveals you, mirrors you, fixes you, and in that way you've already been digested. Do that and the unknowable universe can function through you. In obscurity, it seems to me, polarisations stop, in obscurity there is no praying mantis and prey. There is just the one eternal awareness. The only awareness required of the praying mantis is to know that you are the praying mantis – the greatest and finest ego roaming the Wild West universe.

Conor McKenna

is a trained Process Worker and a founder member of RSPOPUK, working as a psychotherapist and group facilitator. He is based in Edinburgh and the Scottish Borders. Conor has recently completed a book on the relationship between inner and outer realities.

'Festschrift' for Jean-Claude

By Anne Currie

Towering legend of a man
twin heroes bound in modern guise.
Hercules, great laughing giant,
crinkly laugh lines, storm and smile.
A boy who tends his Ma in menial tasks
and clears the Augean stable.
No labour then too small, too large, too low.
Kindly heart expanding,
delicate intellect contracting to the sharp precision of a signal.
And generous Hephaestus, vulcan fiery,
magma surging through his roomy veins,
soft and hard in equal measure.
Toughness and humanity, hand in hand,
the two combined to make the many one.
Paterfamilias, father of a swarm
of children, spawned here by his rigour, adopted into process.
Lodged in my heart somewhere.

With love and hugs for your big birthday, dear Jean-Claude.

Anne Currie
retired from a few roles – psychotherapist, teacher, wife.
Leaping into life as a writer, creative artist in the widest
sense, Trustee of RSPOPUK, and a different sort of spouse.
Thanking the Eternal for Process Work.

Thank You Jean-Claude
An Inner Work on how to show my Appreciation fully

By Amyas Doulton.

When I found out that there was going to be a book written for Jean-Claude about Inner Work to celebrate both his birthday and his work, I really wanted to somehow say "thank you" to Jean-Claude for all his help and encouragement. Therefore I decided to show my appreciation in the form of an Inner Work titled 'Thank You Jean-Claude.'

Before writing this I decided that I wanted to do something along the lines of Zen painting where I would write down everything as it occurred and would not come back to it after I had written. Therefore, I choose to represent each new voice-role (thought) with a new letter of the alphabet. In retrospect I think A is my everyday voice, B an encouraging voice and C a critical voice, though others might see this differently.

A: Thank you Jean-Claude

B: No that's not enough you have got to say why you're thankful.

A: Jean-Claude when I spend time with you I start to feel better and I cannot explain exactly how. But somehow your presence and encouragement brings something I cannot find in myself, and it is this that sorts everything out, makes everything feel possible.

C: Yeah, that's still not enough come on you want to make this article shine above the rest, and you would like Jean-Claude to be both touched and to laugh when he reads it.

A: Ah man, I now feel guilty for saying thanks, and now I don't know what to say.

C: Yeah you do.

A: Okay, there is a part of me that would like me to shine, and would like Jean-Claude to be touched and laugh when he reads this and I want to say more.......

C: But you have gone blank again, well how are you supposed to shine when you have gone blank again.

A: I suppose I want also to say thanks Jean-Claude as you have helped me accept all the parts of me, and when I spend time with you I feel its okay to be me, bad parts included.

B: You still have more to say.

C: Well he does if he wants to shine.

A: Well I would like to say that I would like to be able to do what you have done for me for others. I would like to represent that part that you have represented to me for others, and I can't quite say this.

C: But you just have.

A: Yeah but I feel there is something else, as I notice a tension in my head and shoulders.

C: Well change channels.

A: Well I want to say more but don't know how to express my gratitude fully.

C: Trust your body.

A: I feel quasi-modo emerging, and wants to grunt at you Jean-Claude. Which means 'Hi' and 'Thanks'

B: Who the hell is quasi-modo?

A: It's an ally that Jean-Claude helped me to find.

C: Come on you've said enough, you're taking too long over this and the article is not going to shine if it's too long.

A: Okay maybe I can't express my gratitude fully, but maybe I can start to live it.

C: What do you mean it?

A: Well I mean I can live all the experiences that I am grateful for.

After writing this somebody asked me what I meant by 'live all the experiences that I am grateful for'. To be honest I am not sure what I meant by this, as it was just the first thing that came to me. But on reflection I believe it is to do with a change in attitude that spending time with Jean-Claude helps me to realize. For instance most of the time when I notice a body symptom or have a relationship problem I slip into a kind of victim identity, where I feel miserable, I believe life is unfair, I feel guilty (thinking I have done something wrong), start hating myself, and life and think I am never going to be able to live how I want to. But when I am with Jean-Claude my attitude changes, I start to notice how a symptom or difficulty can be a valuable source of information. Life then has meaning, and feels rewarding. Therefore, I think to 'live all the experiences that I am grateful for' refers to trusting and listening to life or nature, not seeing it as a catastrophe but as a source of growth. Furthermore, if I lived from this point of view I believe it might be a good way of saying thanks to Jean-Claude for his help and encouragement.

Amyas Doulton

was first introduced to Process Work when a friend suggested he read a book by Arnold Mindell, from that point he
has been hooked and is now contemplating becoming a
formal student.

Rivers Deep, Mountains High

By Themis Tocles

I always had the impression that I'm a sea-person, so was trying to repeatedly settle somewhere close to the water, and when that water was not part of a beach, an archipelagos or the ocean, at least a sufficiently wide river would greet my urban journeys daily. I was very embarrasssed when on a rainy Edinburgh afternoon, looking with my therapist for my source of power, I found myself mooring on the top of the Olympus Mountain. I subsequently took to trekking all the Scottish mountains within reach, in order to discover not as much any more what's on a mountain, but rather what's in a mountain. As a result, life was calling forth to my experience all sorts of mountains, included a bizarre one with a Broke Back and another called Jean-Claude, which together with Olympus, all felt to have been a home since time immemorial.

Please, do have a seat and pick up our Ghost, ladies and gentlemen, since first we are going to watch a movie, which according to the international media is about a 'gay love story' in mid '60s America, around the time I was being physically born, elsewhere. The film is called 'Brokeback Mountain'[1], so as every Back in all physical bodies accommodates a secondary process, and here we are dealing with a broke(n) one, chances are that all we are left to deal with is just a primary process. Therefore, all you can choose is how you are going to be dreamed up by an empty jacket hung in a Wyoming closet, with which the film concludes.

In very much the same way we all choose most things in our modern, complacent 'democracies'.

Far out on the screen though, I tend to get a close-up from all the secondary roles of the drama, like in the days of the ancient Greek tragedy, when the Chorus was valued as well as the protagonist. I'm letting my love grow and my smile freeze for all that terror on the face of a desperate housewife at a window, for the wet, frustrated glance of a betrayed widow on a phone, for those estranged children perpetuating misery who are also becoming mine, for those orphan children in the hands of alienating grand-parents like the ones I had once, for edgy bar mates and aggressive bosses I shared, for vulgar boozers and perplexed girl-friends who flirted with my days, for my potential murderers and my promiscuous contacts, for my lovers claiming my spirit and my parents claiming my ashes.

Far within, on my 21st century globalised seat, I'm relishing my fresh, white, middle-class Yankee identity, my own liberation and a 'gay' culture to which to belong, through entrance fees to Back-rooms, where I'll be spending my days off and my wages. When the World Channel[2] covers my ears with the exhilarant San Francisco and western European capitals' tune, I know very well how to move. When an alluring community of body parts celebrates life, while consuming poppers, alcohol and mine, I know who I am. When the heroes of the film are dying in a ditch, or shutting down in a caravan, I won't manage to hold my tears back. For all those people like me, once upon a time ripped by death and isolation. For all those people before me, who never had a chance to realize individuation. For all those people unlike me, who have been stifled by neighbours, peers, relatives and (often conflicting layers of) ancestors.

I'm restless, I need to jump into the screen. It's strange; it feels familiar here, neither like 'the' hero, nor just like a role. All I can see is a huge, blinding projector, erasing the features of the audience. All I can feel is an amalgam of compassion and repulsion, to which I can't relate. From the theatre's far upper boxes, the psychologists call me names: and I can hear, "Oedipus!" Old Age besides New Age spiritual 'Masters' cry me curses: and I 'learn', that even the 'primitives' in the jungle would never believe what, as a man, I 'do' 'to' (but not 'with') other men[3]. And I suddenly know why the Brokeback Mountain kills its stories and its hosts on time, just before the arrival of devious mass saviours, who, by the early '80s, would blur and trade with my Edges, which I last disowned in a mid '70s ditch or caravan. And I suddenly see why I can't cross over to my secondary process, without an Edge to own, as I can see the difference between death and isolation, instead of unconsciously and happily surrendering to both.

But the film isn't interactive, so I get stuck on the full flat-ness of the screen. If I'm Oedipus, you will never know that Laius was my father. Laius, I repeat, the inventor of pederasty and founder of warrior homosexuality. I've neither the means to spell the word 'monocolus' back; that critical stage of the alchemy, when the solar and the lunar energies of the masculine principle unite. I have no power to get the jungle's 'primitives' – as well as fishes, birds, animals and insects - into the 'Masters'' respective parishes and ashrams for a proof. I only have enough 'primitive' connectedness to offer parts of my split persona to the needs of their male aspirants. Since I honour the earth I step on, regardless if I still struggle to comply with a universe of flesh and the ambient erotica. Erotica insults my sense of Eros, as much as my classification as 'Gay' insults my sense of Wholeness, since for the first time in human history a (rather shallow but certainly one-sided) psychological quality has been chosen to describe a part of the World's population, attaching a fixed psychological content to a strictly physical connotation, far beyond any personal or cultural context.

I'm roaring. I'm Inuit and Gambian; I'm Cherokee and Tamil. Get off of my slopes, where my unfinished task of building civilization lies, or I will kill you anyhow! Clear off my Channels, or you will never acquire back immunity! Pull your Trojan Horse out of my Process, or Troy will be scorched earth! Release my Spirit to the plains, or you will perish within seduction. Far up here, life will go on as ever, like the very day of Big Bang, when the receptive and the expressive, the sensory and motor, the feminine and masculine first divided all life processes into two aspects. When the adaptive experience of all living organisms first contained a mixture of these yielding and assertive elements, which, from the universal day one, keep being utilized in exactly the same way: according to their natural predisposition - to prefer one over the other - or as appropriate to particular circumstances

Life seems hilariously absurd, every time I look from the Brokeback Mountain far down to the plains. The Plain Rank seems to know very well how to deal with polarities. If I can think for myself, I will certainly be told what to do, and if I can act on my own, I will definitely be told what to think. Yet there are two great areas of psychic function, where knowledge seems to be suspiciously atrophic. These are the Love and Power capacities, and Sexuality in the area of Love is the analogue of Celebration in the Power realm, two biologically established channels of psychic surplus overflow[4]. There is no aspect of psychological growth, in which the individuals are more on their own than on this journey into the uncharted land of the Brokeback Mountain, where the real issues of human development lie exposed.

Mountains will be mountains though, whereas it's all about the plains: where artificial isolation of the sexual and celebrative capacities, leaves the biggest residue of unattached surplus tendencies, which find outlet in promiscuity and addictive pat-terns. 'Gays' will be 'gays' too, and it's very much about the scope of love and power inter-actions between men and women, dwindling into insignificance, while they unite through their genitals rather than their polarized identities, while men who attempt to love on an independent basis, must face a psycho-logical feminine structure, which they are taught to have re-pulsed. Adults will be adults, as well, but it's very much about children, who refuse to choose that pattern of inner identity, which doesn't best serve their need to put psychic distance between them and the adaptive demands of their family, thus not identified with the parent of the same sex. And cultures will be cultures, remaining rigid from generation to generation, with little or no need for social progress. But, after all, because inner identity rests on masculine-feminine polarity, it's all about everyone and the impossibility to enter upon a life of unrestricted growth without the ability to recognize and use masculine and feminine psychological traits, outside the influence of the socially supported gender roles.

It seems I've been slowly slipping onto the plains, and here's London, a dizzy and uprooting descent like any other trip to flatness. Yet there are some rooms, which shelter Mountains, and I can tell at once, as I sit opposite one, by the name of Jean-Claude. Shortly, a group of people is dreaming of a privilege, whereas our Ghost of a collective wolf is dreaming me up. I can't help feeling my fury building up, while my hurt Anatolia, Mongolia and Sri Lanka welcome thousands of figures, which take me over. I surrender, leaving behind me an empty chair to represent absences as such, as I wander with my broken metacommunicator[5] to the surrounding boulevards. I have a dream to follow, in which I walk away dropping my ethnic guerrilla weapons, wondering where is the difference between a rhinoceros and a unicorn. In Consensus Reality terms, I just follow my steps without purpose, until they stop in front of certain premises called 'the Unicorn Café'.

Far out, from the Unicorn café, I will be witnessing the group working with its absentees, whereas far within, I would be working with mine. The minutes would be revealing an entire mountain chain rising from that room, which would be filling me, as well as all the enraged figures, with huge tidal waves of love and resolution, from the north of London far up to China. I was following that whole process, addressing text messages from a mobile phone to a group member in that room: 3.10 pm, 'oops, that was brilliant', 3.23 pm 'yes, that way, you are all a gang of stars', 3. 38 pm 'thanks, now the figures tell me', which allowed us later to verify how accurate that whole inter-action has been. Shortly before 4 pm, all that was left to discover was why Jean-Claude has been the one, who has never been the target of the figures' fury, although simul-taneously so closely connected to the group, as if non-insular islands do exist.

It's the awareness of the inescapability of doing Inner Work every single instant, as one goes along, breathes, walks and interacts with others, which builds the Mountain material up and turns a single (wo)man more catalysing than an entire system or culture. The awareness of the masculine components in femininity and the feminine components in masculinity, which need to be expressed without upsetting the primacy of the inner identity. The awareness of the impossibility to develop new capacities for intervention in the life of others, without a changing awareness of what the needs of others really are. Even in the moment and especially in the moment. Masculinity accumulates energy, which needs the opportunities that exist in a responsive psychological environment. The discovery of goodness in others comes through the constructive exploitation of their responsiveness. The more such resources are used, the more valuable they become, and in the Process of such exploitation both the user and the used grow in dimensions. Femininity on the other hand, does not become organised for action, until its submissive potential has been realized in surrender to a loved object. The devotional work of love brings balance to the personality, without undermining its tension storing function.

The feminine of the truth seeker, who is guided by love, cannot afford to accept action patterns, until they have been tested in the arena of her own personal devotion to an ideal. The masculine of the seeker of independent moral leadership cannot accept the potential seductions of loyalty, until actual experience has demonstrated that his freedom will not be compromised in the Process. Few hours later, I'm looking for Jean-Claude, who in turn is looking for me in the nearby pubs, because I am not again back to the room, wrestling with whatever I've been forced to swallow since millennia, which ascends from my feet and through my choking throat, in an attempt to evade the confine of a persona and regain the air. As I catch sight of him, walking on that Holloway Road, I re-member the abysmal depths that the Mountain lagoons and rivers bear, onto which I was going to mirror myself, into which I was going to dive, through which I was going to swim and upon which I was later going to surf. After all, I always had the impression that I'm a sea-person for a reason, although it was just a fragment of my higher dream.

Themis Tocles

was born into an atmosphere of Asia Minor, which is neither Greece nor Turkey on the map, yet both in Dreamland. Ever since, he has been studying Life, one way or another, wherever his process led him. Currently a Phase I student of Process Work, joining the UK community from the Scottish Highlands.

[1] *'Brokeback Mountain'*, By Pulitzer Prize Winning Authors, Annie Proulx and Larry McMurtry, Winner of 3 Academy Awards (including Best Director) and Winner of 4 BAFTA Awards (including Best Film) 2006, Directed by Ang Lee, Produced by James Schamus, Production Companies: River Road Entertainment, Focus Features, Ennis Films

[2] Channels: Signal vehicles, which convey intended and unintended communication. There are four irreducible channels: the proprioceptive channel, the visual channel, the auditory channel and the movement (kinaesthetic) channel. There are also two composite channels (made up of a combination of elementary channel experiences), which are the relationship channel and the world channel. (Diamond, J and Jones L.S. (2004) *A Path Made by Walking – Process Work in Practice*, Portland Oregon: Lao Tse Press)

[3] Osho, (1999) *Courage: The Joy Of Living Dangerously*, New York: St Martin's Griffin

[4] Rosenfels, P. (1989) *Homosexuality: The Psychology of the Creative Process*, New York: Ninth Street Center

[5] Metacommunicator: The function of how a person describes their process, which is similar to the concept of the 'detached observer' found in Buddhism. It is a self reflective capacity to notice, organise, and report on ones experiences. Sometimes it is also called a 'witness', 'observer', 'narrator' or 'inner facilitator'. *A Path Made by Walking – Process Work in Practice*. See n.4.

A Baker's Dozen*

By Evelyn Figueroa

Jean-Claude has been a teacher and a model for many Process Work students. Here are 13 things I have learnt from him that inspire me in my work and daily life :

1. Follow your unintentional body movements and go where they take you.
2. Unfold the process behind your symptom, bring its energy to awareness and use it consciously.
3. Believe in what you're feeling. It's part of the field.
4. Go into what scares you.
5. When in a dilemma, metacommunicate about it.
6. If someone projects a figure on you, inhabit it completely.
7. Learn from your critic. Sometimes he/she can be helpful.
8. In a conflict, support yourself completely before taking the other side.
9. Facilitate all sides. That's deep democracy.
10. Life brings challenges. Go inside yourself, do Inner Work and learn from the situation.
11. Be compassionate towards your different inner figures.
12. Pick up the style of the figure that is disturbing you and use it to relate to it.
13. Notice where the energy is in you, what excites and moves you and follow that.

*An English expression relating to bread, which is the staff of life. It refers to the way bread used to be sold.

Trees in the clouds, Kirsten Wassermann

Magical Beginnings

By Edna Holt

In 1987 Arny Mindell came to London and gave the very first weekend seminar in what was then called Process Oriented Psychology. Many people who were there were delighted, challenged and stimulated by this completely new approach to working with people.

In the following spring, Jean-Claude and Arlene gave a seminar in Devon on the theme of 'Deep Bodywork and Spiritual Experience'. My memory of the information booklet was of a picture of mountains and in the paragraphs below, the word 'dreambody' resonated with me. It evoked a sense of excitement and curiosity. I had been in analysis for only a few weeks and had developed the discipline of recording my dreams in a journal. The night before the seminar I dreamt of walking in a large garden that had green lawns and a lotus tree in full bloom on my left hand side.

Arriving at the venue a few minutes late, I drove towards a large country house along a gravel path. There were lawns on either side and a lotus tree in full bloom on my far left. I remember feeling very happy to see it.

Inside a ground floor room I found a circle of people sitting on the floor or on cushions listening to a man who spoke with a French accent. Since my first meeting with Jean-Claude my life has never been the same.

All my professional working life had been spent as a teacher and while I was interested in psychology I had no real idea what psychotherapy was. However as I love to learn I felt pleased and happy to be in this new learning situation. There were a dozen of us and we spent a deep, rich time together in which lasting relationships were forged.

This was my first contact with learning about how our bodies are communicating information all the time and how within us, are dream figures needing our awareness and attention, so that we can become more whole and live life more fully. At the time this was so new and astonishing, as was the idea of bringing our inner world together with the outer world. The seeds of all my future studies were sown at this seminar.

Jean-Claude's rigorous questioning in pursuit of under-standing signals and his accuracy in following the 'dreaming body' was a huge learning for all of us and I personally felt I had come home in this milieu. Working in the middle of the group on an issue and unable to reach a decision, one person looked upwards and muttered "oh God", at which point there were three taps on the French windows, delivered by a magnificently coloured pheasant. There were several such numinous moments that I can remember.

These were the magical beginnings of Process Work in the UK.

Edna Holt
Is a certified Process Worker living in Bristol and has been in Education both mainstream and alternative all her professional life.

Dear Jean-Claude

By Nick Turner

Although I have been attending your seminars for the last ten years, it is only relatively recently that I have got to know you more. As I have grown in my awareness and skills, I have recognised and appreciated your depth of experience and your mastery, in all its breadth, courage and sensitivity, of your skills and metaskills. This is so apparent when I listen and re-listen to my few audio recordings of sessions with you. Each time I hear something new and something old which I need to be reminded of.

You teach me the importance and meaning of being aware of what is happening in oneself in the moment, and how that is related to the process of other person, the group around me and the world. By being aware of yourself, and bringing yourself into the process, you model so eloquently that metaskill. You have often become a touchstone for my secondary process, rarely in my dreams, mostly in my everyday reality. As I close my eyes right now and think of you, I see you in my mind's eye and see various facets. I see the care and sensitivity, the way you look with your eyes and your heart into the signals and the essence of the other person. I want to thank you from the bottom of my heart for seeing, supporting and encouraging the diversity within me and not holding back on telling me what you perceive I most need to learn!

Much love, Nick

Nick Turner
is a Phase II Process Work student, who has a private practice in East Grinstead and London. His special interests include shamanism, organisations, and discovering new ways to lead a creative everyday life.

Melting the Ice with Jean-Claude

By Sally Olsberg

During the long years of my training in Process Work I was plagued by frozen states. They were such a problem I truly wondered whether I would be able to fulfil the requirements of passing my exams despite all my hard work and single minded devotion.

By frozen states I mean a kind of trance in which one hardly notices that one is altered relative to ordinary reality. They are shock reactions to traumatic events from the past which can be reactivated in the moment. They are often associated with physical trauma or abuse situations where the person feels unable to defend themselves directly at the time so that the body and mind create a dissociation from the situation as a protection from feeling the fear of annihilation. When one is in a new stressful situation or even unconsciously reminded for some reason of previous trauma, the frozen state can recur. They are called frozen states because fear creates an almost shut down of sensation, a petrifaction or turning to stone.

This kind of reactivation happened to me often during my training (still does from time to time in unexpectedly stressful or frightening situations) and especially when working in the therapist role in front of peers and teachers during training supervision. Something about putting myself on trial created the kind of terror which put me into a frozen state.

The nature of frozen states is to dull awareness so that it's hard from the inside to notice it's happening. Other people could see it in me. I might go silent and have a far away look or try to carry on as though nothing was different (perhaps a way I'd learnt to deal with some of the difficult experiences of my childhood and adolescence, that is, carrying on as if nothing bad was happening) but of course any interventions I made just didn't seem to work as my client knew at some level that I wasn't really present.

When working in front of Jean-Claude, I was often even more frozen than ever, probably because I held him in such respect and awe that I really wanted to impress him with my work, thus creating an even bigger pressure on myself. Of course he saw right away that I was frozen. Time and again he gently intervened, showing me a myriad of new patterns for helping me out of it. Sometimes he'd get me to step out and look at myself. He'd stand with me, his big presence next to me, a warm big hand on my shoulder. Above all, it was the power and warmth of his love that showed me how to defrost myself, how to truly trust my feelings that were hidden under that layer of deep set ice. His love and belief in me modelled how to be towards myself, and the tears would fall, tears of sorrow, joy and relief.

Looking back I marvel at the patience he must have had. He could so easily have got fed up with me seeming to be getting nowhere and not even noticing how frozen I was. But he was always there for me, through thick and thin, year in, year out, always teaching me my craft and believing I'd make it somehow:- How to recognise the signals when I was frozen, those subtle changes in my awareness and sense of reality, and how to work with myself lovingly when I noticed it happening.

Jean-Claude then became for me an inner figure too, a powerful and loving spirit who warmed those frozen states, melting them with love and kindness. That inner figure is still with me, standing by me, a big solid hand on my back, protect-ting and loving me yet urging me to bring my awareness to everything inside and outside of me, however disturbing.

A most wonderful moment for me was when I worked in front of Jean-Claude at my final Process Work exams in which I did a particularly fluid and unfrozen piece of work with a couple. There were tears in his eyes when he proudly recognised how far I'd come from those early days, and I was proud too of my achievement and in awe of the Tao which had brought me such a teacher.

Thank you Jean-Claude.

Sally Olsberg
is a certified Process Worker practising in Manchester and Hebden Bridge, West Yorkshire. She is currently writing a process oriented guide to recovery from addictions, working title 'A Pot too Hot'.

Jean-Claude - It was you...

It was you who turned me on to Process Work with Inner Work at Unstone Grange in April 1990.

1. 'First - meditate as you normally do:'
   Whew! I'm OK as I am.
2. 'Are you seeing, hearing, feeling?'
   Wow! This is new
3. 'Now - notice what disturbs you.'
   Help! Am I ready to face that role - Acknowledge the one who wants control?

The wondrous Jean-Claude. That's how you've always been for me. The ultimate in warmth, loving acceptance and consistent loyalty, offering learning, golden learning and ever more delicious learning - and then the toughness sometimes even roughness. And the challenges that keep me growing.

Jean-Claude, I just love you!

Happy 60th Birthday

And a big hug from Sue x

Viel Vergnügen für die nächste Stufe Dein´ ereignisvoll´ Reise.

Sue Holden
psychotherapist and Tai Chi teacher, living in Richmond, North Yorkshire, lover of Process Work, Trustee of RSPOPUK and currently excited by Kite Festival she is organising.

A First Encounter

By Evelyn Figueroa

Sitting on the floor, next to a lady who is lying on her back, going into her inner visions, I am moved; touched by her sadness and the tears that are pouring down her face. This is my first Process Work seminar and as I sit there, I do not know that in a few minutes this lady is going to introduce me to one of her inner dream figures, to her vision of a man who will become my therapist, my teacher and later on a colleague and a friend. And who is essential for her at the moment.

Out of her tears her painful story unfolds and then she laughs, a moment of respite. I am curious and so I ask her about it. She replies she has just had an image of the facilitator of a previous Process Work seminar she had attended. She describes him : 'He is a big man, solid, strong, grounded. He is Swiss and speaks English with a French accent. He has the solidity of the Swiss mountains. There is something tough in him and yet his eyes are soft, full of tenderness.'

I see her smiling. She now looks joyful as she goes further into her inner vision and dreams on. She adds: 'I wish I could get a hug from this man. In my dream he puts his arms around me and just holds me. A feeling of comfort and compassion invades me. It connects me with a very quiet and spacious part inside myself'.

She smiles again. I join her in this tranquil, inner space. Afterwards I ask her what the name of the man is. 'Jean-Claude Audergon', she replies.

As I recall this first encounter with Jean-Claude as someone else's inner dream figure, I realize that part of his essence, that inspires and touches most of us deeply and is a fundamental part of his teaching was in that lady's description. And I, like her, can only smile.

Thank you, Jean-Claude.

Conversations on Co-Facilitation

By Jean-Claude[1] and Arlene Audergon

In addition to the more personal aspects of our relationship, our relationship has been a ground for our creativity and our co-facilitation. Anup Karia and Stanya Studentova invited and inspired us to have a conversation about what it's like to work together.

Arlene: People often ask us about what it's like to facilitate together, as partners. It's a big question. At the heart of Process Work is this interplay between growing in one's personal awareness and how this hangs together with facilitating within the fields we are in. When working together, particularly over time, there is the added interplay between our awareness in relationship, and facilitating as a team.

Over the years we've also both had a big interest in how the process of individuation - the journey of grappling with what it means to become oneself - hangs together with being deeply involved in relationship, and in the world. When we first met, you were writing a thesis on 'Individuation and Communication'- I remember wonderful conversations we had.

Jean-Claude: A lot of people are curious about working together with someone so closely. They often say that they have the experience that when they work together with someone they end up fighting or in competition.

Arlene: People are sometimes a bit surprised by how we bump up against each other so openly when we work together.

Jean-Claude: It creates a spark, that we use to discover what is coming up individually, in relationship, and in the fields we are working. We work consistently at our 'edges'[2] of identity, and on our transference issues with each other over time. Meanwhile, we know "what bugs me is me"[3] and it may also be relevant to the other, and to the field we are in, and if we follow it with awareness, we go right back to the sentient source[4] of things. When we have difficulties in the middle of a project, we are a team, and we know that what comes up in us personally and in our relationship is a motor for creativity, for our facilitation, and for the group or organisation where we are working.

Arlene: For the forum recently in East London on issues facing asylum seekers, refugees, and settled groups, the preparation was so rich, together with our co-facilitators and an active organising group[5]. We found the issues we expected to meet in the forum as they came up inside us. At one level this had to do with meeting our own personal and family history – for example, my parents were refugees, fleeing for their lives from the Holocaust in Germany. After working on that a lot and 'burning wood'[6], I try to use my sensitivity about issues of exclusion and inclusion in my facilitation. Or the way your family was treated, being among the poorest families in the city where you grew up in Switzerland, and how you have worked on that personal history in many ways, and it makes you sensitive about the importance of valuing one another in community.

At another level, preparation is really a moment to moment practice of awareness, finding one's orientation, even in the midst of heated situations. At that forum there was this surprising moment near the end, when we asked this man, a Somali refugee, about his smile. He had been representing the role of the English person who was downing and suspicious, but there was this smile. When we asked if he could say what it was about, he shared his utter joy in being in this multicultural forum, able to engage about such important issues so openly. That touched off a celebratory feeling in everyone there, such a pride in being a multicultural society, which was at the core of the process that evening. We could have almost missed that smile, because we were dealing with such serious and painful issues. Facilitating meant having familiarity with a range of issues and emotions, including trauma from war and violence, the pain of exclusion, fear, prejudice and nationalism, but also the freedom to catch the spark of joy, pride and hope in our multicultural city.

Jean-Claude: Another important basis of facilitating is familiarity with extreme states[7]. Having explored our own extreme states makes things easier – people don't often realize the importance of knowing their own extreme states when facilitating others, particularly in situations with a lot of tension or conflict. Knowing your extreme states allows you to support people to go into those extreme emotions, and it frees you to discover the underlying creative process, instead of only reacting to the outrage or pain or whatever you might be afraid of.

It's useful to keep in mind the basic idea that what you are afraid of in a group is 'you'. You are projecting the part of you that you have no relationship to. So, if you fear something – you know that you are going to learn something about yourself, and you are also onto something that needs to be processed in the group. People are often afraid of intense emotions, attacks, critics, etc.

Unfolding these emotions also in our personal relationship has allowed us to facilitate the field we are in, instead of being frozen, or taken in by those feelings. I remember going by train to an organisation where we consult sometimes, and we got into this wild conflict, and then realized that what we were experiencing was 'dreamed up'[8]. The people in that organisation had huge conflicts and no patterns how to have conflicts directly.

Arlene: When we go to facilitate somewhere, we tend to work on whatever relationship issue might come up in us, and then we stop and notice the polarization we were dealing with and any resulting transformation – all this becomes useful information when we arrive on the job. That day on the train, what was so important was the style of having strong conflict together. That freed our awareness to not be shy to support the group to bring out the intensity of their conflicts with each other, even though they are a group so devoted to peace.

Having quite a bit of fluidity in our relationship makes it easier to support the people we are working with. One way to look at this is: the process doesn't really belong to anyone. It's not really your process or mine, or the organisation's.

Jean-Claude: It's the inherent creativity in the field seeking expression through all these dynamics. Our training is to try to hone our awareness to facilitate moment to moment, at these different levels, with respect for the given context.

Arlene: Facilitating brings awareness into the field – not only to ease tensions but to perceive and bring out the inherent creativity that is implicit there.

Jean-Claude: You sense a field when you enter it – you sense its tension and its creativity both – you feel the atmosphere, your reactions to that atmosphere, and its impact on those associated with it. Some talk about a group 'spirit'. In Process Work, we talk about the 'dreaming' field[9].

Facilitating is an awareness practice - we've been talking about the importance of constant learning and training of moment to moment perception, including familiarity with our own personal history, extreme states, and discovering how all this hangs together with the creative field we are entering. We saw Ilya Prigogine on a video speaking so beautifully about what it's like to be in a world in which "we are at all times embedded in what we are describing"[10]. Process Work facilitation methods help make it possible to observe and intervene in the field - differentiating the polarization of roles and ghost roles[11]; awareness of rank dynamics[12]; thinking and intervening systemically[13]; noticing 'hot spots'[14] as the points of potential escalation, but also points of potential transformation; noticing 'cool spots'[15]; and accurately following the feedback of individuals and groups in the dimensions of consensus reality, dreaming and sentience[16].

Arlene: With these concepts and tools and with a co-facilitator by your side, we can kind of jump into the field and explore, knowing in the spirit of 'deep democracy'[17] that it is the whole field that will be wise, if there can be a facilitated interaction among all the parts. When cofacilitating, the field is moving us along with the group. Whatever you or your partner is doing is part of the field that needs facilitating. If your partner does something surprising, outside what you would expect, you may feel – oh oh – why is he doing that??? But as a team-mate you just keep facilitating, and might notice the role he is representing. Or if you reacted to it, what is the other role? You immediately see and act on your perception in view of a larger process. And your partner does the same for you. We each facilitate ourselves, each other, and the group or the field as we perceive it.

Jean-Claude: That's so important. Using Arny's method of vectors or getting in touch with the underlying sentient dimension[18] is also useful in getting to the essence of our teamwork and that brings a lot of freedom as well as an orientation to the underlying creative processes within the groups and organisations we enter. When co-facilitating, another important issue is style - what to do if your partner has a completely different style?

Arlene: Sometimes I really just feel it's a question of enjoying style differences.

Jean-Claude: But, some people will ask how do we enjoy it, rather than just feeling irritated.

Arlene: I guess it's getting to know and appreciate our own styles and what Arny used to call our 'anti-styles' and having some compassion for our quirks - getting to know our own deepest nature and enjoying the nature of others. It's like being on a journey – enjoying the richness and diversity when there is not just one style dominating

Jean-Claude: You're describing an attitude of appreciating diversity. It's love – love for the unknown, and I feel it's love for your partner, too, and for the field's diversity, for what might just happen. You could also say that the disturbing style is just what is needed in the situation, and your love for the process, and your eldership, and interest in the whole process, is what guides you and your partner in those moments.

Arlene: At the same time, if style difference is disturbing one thing we might do is find out if there are issues around style and culture in the organisation we are working. Appreciating the group's diversity of styles is a central thing to remember at any time.

Jean-Claude: You're talking about facilitating what comes up, rather than identifying with the position of facilitator. That brings an incredible sense of ease when co-facilitating together.

214

Arlene: I get excited by what you are saying about ease. Maybe it's because I don't often think about facilitation in terms of 'ease'! Even when a situation is difficult, or we get stuck, or in conflict with each other, there is this constant orientation and experience of welcoming and processing what arises, and this is the background ease you are talking about.

Jean-Claude: You sense a tension, a 'hot spot', a 'ghost', or the patterns of communication that are cycling in a group or organisation - What makes it effortless is that you welcome the process by framing and entering the difficulties. Chinese philosophy calls this kind of ease, 'wuwei', or effortless action.

The same is true for relationship. You consistently meet difficulties, and these are the expression of your 'pilot wave'[19], the guiding force of your individuation, and the underlying 'myth' or 'dream' shaping your partnership. A myth shaping our relationship has been 'David and Goliath'. It came up in that work we did together at one of Arny's early relationship seminars some 20 years ago.

Arlene: That myth has been important for our personal relationship, and also for our creative work and cofacilitation. One way I understand it is that Goliath represents the challenges of life, and the way we challenge ourselves and one another, and David represents a quality of persistence, gentleness and love, in being able to meet those challenges with some ease.

Jean-Claude: It makes me think about how, as a facilitator, it's important to work on one's relationship to long-term hard-ships. Rather than feeling blocked by them or blocking others - that means welcoming those parts of oneself that may not be so likeable.

Arlene: You mentioned 'pilot wave' I like Arny's use of this term to describe that sense of deepest direction manifesting throughout our life. While that pilot wave expresses itself through wonderful experiences in our lives, it almost certainly also appears in our most difficult and seemingly intractable problems that shape us.

Jean-Claude: That's why we even need facilitators to facilitate the problematic, polarized and painful issues people have and need support for and a dedication to processing one's growing edges and individuation.

Arlene: There's a tendency in so many of us to suffer from the problem of supporting our nature only where we feel its palatable….and we all need to find support to love our nature, including the most troublesome bits.

Jean-Claude: You are talking about such a central aspect of facilitation – a metaskill that can welcome processes as they come. Amy described 'metaskills'[20] as the conscious use of the feelings and attitudes with which we use skills. All of the skills and the practice of Process Work spring from this underlying service and dedication to process, that Arny always models.

Arlene: He constantly models learning from nature, moment to moment to moment.

Jean-Claude: It's that continual discipline or practice that brings the sense of ease we were talking about.

Arlene: It's like when someone asked Jung if he believed in God, and he said "it's not a matter of belief."

Jean-Claude: There is no real secret to that kind of familiarity – it's like you feel at ease speaking French, if you speak it everyday. You grow in your ability to facilitate yourself and others, and the field moving all of us – you learn from doing it - from the encounter.

Jean-Claude Audergon, Lic.Phil. I
practises and teaches Process Work internationally; co-founder of training in Zurich, Portland, RSPOPUK, Community Force for Change and the Arts Atelier; author 'The Body in Process Work', chapter in Totton N (Ed) *New Dimensions in Body Psychotherapy*, London: Open University Press/ McGraw 2005. www.processwork-audergon.com

Arlene Audergon, Ph.D.
co-founded RSPOPUK, and CFOR Community Force for Change, teaching and practising Process Work internationally; Author of *The War Hotel: Psychological dynamics in violent conflict*, Whurr/Wiley 2005, and articles and chapters on conflict resolution, collective trauma, theatre and mental health. She co-directed SPIRIT with Improbable Theatre. www.processwork-audergon.com

1   At the time of writing Jean-Claude did not know that this article was going to be published in the book dedicated to him.

2   The 'edge', a central concept in Process Oriented Psychology refers to a belief system that defines an identity. It is a limit to our known identity or worldview– Over the 'edge' is an emerging process or pattern. See Mindell A, (1987) *The Dreambody in Relationships*, London: Routledge, p.47-55,

3   'Me' and 'Not me' refers to our identity and that which appears as disturbing or 'other'. Mindell talks about what 'bugs' you in creating the irritation necessary sometimes for awareness.

4   An underlying unity and generative creativity has been described in different ways by many philosophies and spiritual systems. Mindell describes the 'sentient' realm that precedes the differentiation of polarities and dreaming. See Mindell A. (2000*) Dreaming while awake. Techniques for 24-hour lucid dreaming* Charlottesville: Hampton Roads. p. 36

5   The forum, 'Home and Refuge: an evening discussion on community issues related to Asylum and Migration', was co-facilitated by Anup Karia and Olufemi Hughes together with Arlene and Jean-Claude Audergon. The forum was organised by CFOR (Community Force for Change) and Community Health Centre, Waltham Forest PCT. The organising group included Stanya Studentova, Nick Turner, Gina Clayton, Mike Fitter, Iona Fredenburgh, Louise Warner, Amyas Doulton, Kerri Cripps, Olufemi Hughes, and Anup Karia, as well as Nihad Fathi, Lela Husein and Nasim Patel.

6   Mindell A (1992) *Leader as Martial Artist*, San Francisco: Harper Collins, p.5

7   Mindell A (1988) *City Shadows: Psychological Interventions in Psychiatry*, Routledge,. See also Mindell A (1995) *Sitting in the Fire: Large Group Transformation using conflict and diversity*, Portland: LaoTse Press, p. 103

8   'Dreamed up' refers to the tendency for the facilitator to behave like a part of the field, often that part which is over the edge of identity of the individual or group you are working with. See Mindell A (1987) *The Dreambody in Relationships*, Routledge, p.34-35

9   See Mindell A (1992*) Leader as Martial Artist*, San-Francisco, Harper Collins, p. 11-20

10   Ilya Prigogine in ' *The Chaotic Universe'*, Art Meets Science, Part II, Mystic Fire Video

[11] Mindell A (1992) *Leader as Martial Artist*, n.6 p. 23 See also Audergon A (2005) *The War Hotel: Psychological Dynamics in Violent Conflict*, London: Whurr/ Wiley, p.166

[12] See Mindell A (1995) *Sitting in the Fire*, n 7

[13] Process Work has contributed to systems theory with its concept of how conflicts are polarized and cycle, and how conflicts can transform or evolve at the system 'edge' and 'hot spot'.

[14] Hot Spots are moments of charge and sensitivity. Conflicts cycle and escalate at hot spots. Hot spots are also doorways to transforming conflict. See Mindell A (1995) P27, 41-42 See also Audergon A (2005), p. 273-277

[15] A 'cool spot' is a moment of momentary resolution, de-escalation, or shift in understanding. See Mindell A, www.aamindell.net

[16] Diamond J, & Jones L S. (2004) *A Path Made by Walking. Process Work in Practice*. Portland. Oregon. LaoTse Press. p. 73-77. See also Audergon Jean-Claude, (2005) 'The Body in Process Work', Chapter in Totton N (Ed) *New Dimensions in Body Psychotherapy*, London: Open University Press/ McGraw

[17] Mindell A (1992) *Leader as Martial Artist*. p. 154-156

[18] Mindell A (2000) *Quantum Mind*. Lao Tse Press. p 285

[19] Mindell uses Bohm's term Pilot Wave to refer to this underlying direction and orientation. Mindell, A. (2004) *The Quantum Mind and Healing*, Charlottesville: Hampton Roads, p. 74-76

[20] Mindell, Amy, (1995) *Metaskills: The Spiritual Art of Therapy*, Tempe, Arizona: New Falcon Publications

Yummy Carrot Cake for Jean-Claude

By Marina O'Connell

I happen to know you like this cake and it is healthy, too (kind of!). I hope you find time to make and enjoy it.

8 oz plain flour
2 tsp baking powder
1 tsp cinnamon
4 eggs
8 oz sugar
8 fl oz sunflower oil
12 oz grated carrots
4 oz chopped walnuts

Beat together the eggs, sugar and oil, add carrots and nuts. Then add flour, baking powder and cinnamon.

Stir well. Lily-mei (my daughter) is very good at this bit.

Pour mixture into a baking tin and cook at 180° C or gas mark 4 for 30-50 minutes until a knife inserted into the centre of the cake comes out clean.

Decorate with a dusting of icing sugar.

Eat… yum yum.

Marina O'Connell

is an organic fruit grower and has taught gardening and sustainabilty for 20 years. She studied Process Work and has applied this to her environmental work and gardening, and uses this to teach ecopsychology. She is a mother to two gorgeous girls